4dspace:
Interactive Architecture
Guest-edited by Lucy Bullivant

Since the Industrial Revolution and the rise of science fiction, the popular impulse has often been to regard technology as a socially derisive and potentially malign force. In the 1990s, this was further exaggerated by the spectre of cyberspace with its promise of the domination of the virtual over the physical. It engendered visions of a horrific netherworld responded to by even the most subconscious of neuro twitches. This issue of ⌀ turns these angst-ridden visions on their head. Here, spatial design skills and adept application of digital technologies are pooled to aid interaction. This presents technology as a tool for exchange, cohesion and communication. Web and remote technologies may be the props of the contemporary world, but it is the underlying social forces of individualism and an unrelenting work culture that most often distance us from each other, rather than the gadgetry in our hands.

Taking the form of installations and public art, interactive spaces and structures can offer a welcome respite. This is most often as an entertaining diversion, whether it relies on spectacle, wonder or unadulterated fun. The interaction between viewer and what is viewed can be physical or remote, whether the object reponds to a bodily presence or an electronic device such as a mobile phone. At every level, it encourages us to leave our isolated self and interact with a greater social group, perhaps merely for the joy of seeing a chandelier reverberate with light in a gallery, or contributing to an interactive sculpture on an urban scale.

Interaction is not just confined to the art world. It provides tenable and, very often, remarkable solutions for the work place, leisure sector, retail and the domestic. As Mike Weinstock acknowledges in his recollection of EM Forster's refrain 'Only connect!', connection has to be consciously sought out and worked towards. He gives the example of UN Studio's Möbius House, where the architecture enfolds the family in a continuous surface that takes in shared and separate living spaces, enabling the occupants to be simultaneously alone and together. ⌀

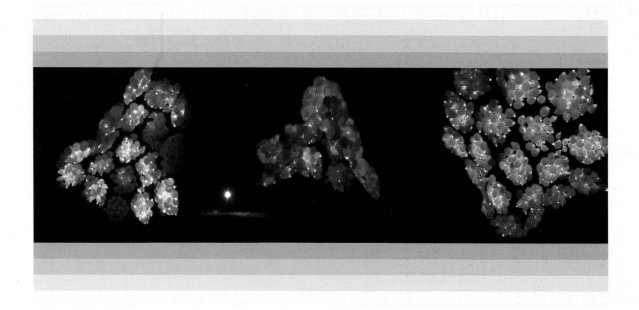

Above
Usman Haque, Sky Ear,
Belluard Bollwerk
International Festival,
Fribourg, Switzerland, and the
National Maritime Museum,
Greenwich, London, July
and September 2004
Sky Ear, designed by architect
and artist Usman Haque,
is made up of hundreds of
glowing helium balloons.
From it are suspended mobile
phones, electromagnetic
sensors that respond to
electromagnetic radiation,
triggering LED lights.

4dspace investigates the reality that the perceptual boundaries between the virtual and physical worlds have been broken, and asks how architecture and its tasks can creatively adopt a fourth dimension, that of digital technologies. Their time-based nature is increasingly producing sociospatial effects that challenge architecture's traditional identity. Meanwhile, the strategies the designers and architects featured in this issue have made their chosen domain of activity seek to constitute a new threshold between the virtual and the physical.

What's clear is that, independent of architecture, this fourth dimension is already inexorably transforming the previously understood identity of space, as a penumbra of new technologies – WiFi and other features of pervasive computing like Bluetooth, RFID tags and GPS – support the spatialisation of time. After a decade or more of the Internet being regarded as an alternative world, now virtual networks are generally perceived as an enhancement to the multidimensionality of the real world. 'Multi-mediated' interactive design is already entering every domain of public and private life as a spatial medium, revolutionising and reinventing our work, leisure and domestic spaces. Social contexts are dominated by the blurring of boundaries between work and play, information retrieval and use. However, as Malcolm McCullough, author of *Digital Ground*,[1]

published in 2004, points out, pervasive technology does not obviate the human need for place.

Experimental strategies have given birth to unique and profoundly moving ways of navigating and occupying space as a social interactive medium.

Treating digital media as physical matter, as does the young Hungarian architect Adam Somlai-Fischer, or harnessing the natural invisible electromagnetism of our environment via mobile phones and SMS – as does London-based Usman Haque in his recent Sky Ear project (see images here, and pages 8–12) – these are activities that through interactive design reinvent our perception of space. Some works present their messages within the gallery context but are anything but hermetic in their implications; for example, Mark Hansen and Ben Rubin's Listening Post, which draws on the human connections made in Internet chat rooms. Many are designed for a range of public places. They build layers of potential personalisation into a context that makes the human response a constantly active and evolving interface. This emerging agenda for interactive architecture and design is about creating not just personal metaphors, but also tactics that create 'different systems of spatiotemporal reference', as Antonino Saggio describes it. On one level, interactive architects and designers are in fact responding to the question posed in the 1960s by Cedric Price: What if a building or space could be constantly generated and regenerated?

To achieve this, multidisciplinary teamwork between architects and designers, working on integrated design

solutions that have always underscored the relationship between design and technology distinguish architect and designer Ron Arad's activities in the field of four-dimensional installations. This creative activity is only the latest stage of a longstanding relationship between design and technology which produces artefacts that are 'bespoke', countering mass-production, he points out. Arad, like the German architects realities:united, designers of the BIX media skin of the Kunsthaus Graz, favours low-res tactics in order to achieve appropriate, affordable, as well as poetic and more subliminal, effects, harnessing emotion rather than technology. At the same time, these tactics are programmed to be adjustable.

The dream of connectivity challenges the traditional demarcating role of architecture, as Ole Bouman points out in his autobiographical essay. The discipline has to face 'a blow to the very stuff it is made of – matter, space and human relations'. But, if, as he says, 'it is people who are now the interface', this inevitably raises issues of what forms of interface they want to function as or negotiate with others. Design can steer many forms of objectives, including social behaviours. The marketing mantra of 'connectivity' is about productivity as workers, but what are the social impacts of being able to avoid the homogeneity entailed in that particular definition? I look at this challenge in my article 'Intelligent Workspaces: Crossing the Threshold'.

Mike Weinstock argues that the *terrain vague* in which we currently live on a domestic level is now a place of transit, a threshold between digital and physical worlds, and that the 'coupling of space, technology and domesticity is part of our architectural legacy'. New technologies are the means to achieving

Above, right and opposite
Sky Ear lift-off, National Maritime Museum, Greenwich, above the Queen's House and the Royal Observatory, 2004
The balloons climbed to a height of over 100 metres, watched by an audience of over 3,500. The green line in the sky is the GMT laser line that is switched on every evening.

systems, with a wide range of specialists brought in as necessary, is vital to confront new social and technological realities, as Walter Aprile and Stefano Mirti, representing Interaction-Ivrea, an educational institution founded in 2001, in Italy, underline in their essay. In their work ethos, all the projects in this issue represent this ambition, with schemes such as the Media House, generated by a Spanish multidisciplinary team led by architects Metapolis, and the Design Research Lab of the Architectural Association's Corporate Fields, exploring the development of team-based interactive activities.

The release of such latent, novel forms of beauty – aural, visual and generated by physical movements or natural phenomena – constitutes a new form of design DNA realised through the agency of digital technologies. *4dspace*, which is developed from a two-day conference of the same name I curated and staged at the Institute of Contemporary Arts, London, in May 2004,[2] studies what motivates these experiments. It also gives insights into how a wide range of cross-disciplinary collaborations are developed, and the cultural, social and technical criteria applied. Architect and artist Christian Moeller took his cue 13 years ago from the burgeoning discipline of media art, while 'low-res'

AD Architectural Design

4dspace:

Interactive Architecture

Guest-edited by Lucy Bullivant

Y-ACADEMY

AD

Architectural Design
Vol 75 No 1 Jan/Feb 2005

ISBN 0470090928
Profile No 173

Editorial Offices
International House
Ealing Broadway Centre
London W5 5DB
T: +44 (0)20 8326 3800
F: +44 (0)20 8326 3801
E: architecturaldesign@wiley.co.uk

Editor
Helen Castle

Production
Mariangela Palazzi-Williams

Art Direction/Design
Christian Küsters (CHK Design)

Design Assistant
Hannah Dumphy (CHK Design)

**Project Coordinator
and Picture Editor**
Caroline Ellerby

Advertisement Sales
01243 843272

Abbreviated positions:
b=bottom, c=centre, l=left, r=right

Front and back cover: Ben Rubin (EAR Studio)
and Mark Hansen, The Listening Post, Whitney
Museum of American Art, New York, 2002.
Photo © Ben Rubin

AD
pp 5, 8(t&bl) & 9 © Usman Haque; pp 6-7 & 8(tr) © Usman Haque, photos Ai Hasegawa; pp 10-11 © Usman Haque, photos Shade Abdul; pp 12 & 13(t,tr &b) © Klein Dytham Architecture, photos Katsuhisa Kida; p 13(tl&c) © Klein Dytham Architecture, photos Jun Takagi; pp14-19 courtesy Ole Bouman; p 20(t&bl) © Usman Haque, photos Pletts Haque; p 20(br) © Usman Haque, photo Sam Brooks; p 21 © Dunne & Raby; p 22(l) courtesy British Telecom; p 22(r) © dESIGN-UC ?????; p 23-6 © R&Sie/Philippe Parreno; pp 27-9 © DECOi images; p 30 © Ivan Gasparini; pp 32-7 © Walter Aprile; p 40 © Arup; p 41 © i.Tech; p 42(t) © Shona Kitchen & Ab Rogers, photos Dan Stevens; pp 42(b) & 43 © IDEO; p 44(t) © SmartSlab Ltd; p 43(b) © Zaha Hadid Architects; p 45 © Archiram/Robert Cohen; pp 46 & 47(t) © Christian Richters; p 47(b) © UN Studio; pp 48 & 49 courtesy Michael Weinstock; pp 51-3 © Metapolis, photos Laura Cantarella; p 54 © Ron Arad Associates, photo Carlos Lavatori; pp 55-6 © Ron Arad Associates, photos Tom Vack; pp 57-61 © Ron Arad Associates; p 62 © Christian Moeller; p 63 courtesy Christian Moeller, photos Ivan Nemec; pp 64(t) & 65(l) courtesy Christian Moeller, photos Masao Yamamoto; p 64(b) courtesy Christian Moeller, photo Sagae Oguma; p 65(r) courtesy Christian Moeller, photos Dieter Leistner; pp 66-7 courtesy Christian Moeller; pp 68-71 © NOX/Lars Spuybroek; pp 72-78 © Tobi Schneidler; pp 79 & 80(c&b) © Jason Bruges Studio Ltd, photo 3DW; p 80(t) © Jason Bruges Studio Ltd; p 81 © 3DW & Jason Bruges Studio Ltd; pp 82(t) & 85 courtesy realities:united, Berlin, photos Landesmuseum Joanneum,

Graz, 2003; pp 82(b) & 83(l) courtesy © realities:united, Berlin, photos Harry Schiffer, Graz; pp 83(t&c) & 84 © realities:united, Berlin; p 83(b) courtesy realities:united, Berlin, photo Piclerwerke GmbH/ArGe, 2003; p 86(l) © Paul Verschure; pp 86(r), 87 & 88(t) © Kynan Eng, ETH Zurich, photos Kynan Eng; pp 88(c&b) & 89 © Kynan Eng, ETH Zurich, photos Stefan Kübli; p 90 © Ben Rubin, photo Evan Kafka; pp 92-3 © Ben Rubin, photos courtesy of the artists; pp 94-6 © ETALAB & Virtual Artists, 2002; pp 97-9 © aether architecture.

AD+
pp 100-02 © Jeff Goldberg/Esto; pp 103, 106 & 109(tr&b) © HG Esch; p 107(tl) © Mels van Zutphen; pp 108-10 © Jane Briginshaw; pp 111-16 © William E Massie, photos Jeremy Oldham and William E Massie; pp 117-24 © Denise Ho Architects; pp 125-27 © Sue Barr.

Acknowledgement
Lucy Bullivant would like to thank the Arts Council of England for awarding her a grant for feasibility research to help develop the concept for this issue.

Subscription Offices UK
John Wiley & Sons Ltd.
Journals Administration Department
1 Oldlands Way, Bognor Regis
West Sussex, PO22 9SA
T: +44 (0)1243 843272
F: +44 (0)1243 843232
E: cs-journals@wiley.co.uk

Printed in Italy by Conti Tipocolor.
All prices are subject to change without notice. [ISSN: 0003-8504]

AD is published bi-monthly and is available to purchase on both a subscription basis and as individual volumes at the following prices.

Single Issues
Single issues UK: £22.99
Single issues outside UK: US $45.00
Details of postage and packing charges available on request

Annual Subscription Rates 2005
Institutional Rate
Print only or Online only: UK £175/ US $290
Combined Print and Online: UK £193/ US $320
Personal Rate
Print only: UK £99/ US $155
Student Rate
Print only: UK £70/ US $110

Prices are for six issues and include postage and handling charges. Periodicals postage paid at Jamaica, NY 11431. Air freight and mailing in the USA by Publications Expediting Services Inc, 200 Meacham Avenue, Elmont, NY 11003

Postmaster
Send address changes to AD Publications Expediting Services, 200 Meacham Avenue, Elmont, NY 11003

topographic and environmental changes to architectural space and, via distributed intelligence and active material systems, living space that changes its internal parameters and performance in direct response to inhabitants' lives and external events is possible. Interactive designer Tobi Schneidler, whose personal long-distance relationship prompted the design of Remote Home, believes that interaction and network technologies will engender a new design thinking about the identity of connected, real-world spaces. Another major project from the last few years that explored this potential is the Media House.

In the next few years, emerging practices in interactive architecture will continue to intervene in the urban environment. War has come to be fought and projected virtually as well as physically; commerce relies on the fourth dimension of the spatialisation of time achieved through dislocated virtual connectivity. How can architecture, design and the urban environment not play a role in such a fundamental redefinition of human relations? We should at the very least demand that a pervasive homogeneity in social spaces be countered by localised strategies.

Various media inform interactive design strategies. An example is the virtual networks by which information and data is received, a creative trigger for the ICE info-lounge designed by KDa and Toshio Iwai. Some media forms – like film – have seemingly galloped ahead with visions architects and designers may or may not subscribe to. Contributors Walter Aprile and Stefano Mirti, whose essay illuminates the commitment to interactive design and architecture at the Interactive Ivrea Institute in Italy, an educational institution founded in 2001, admit that they love indulging in the great British tradition of science and social fiction dating back to Thomas More's *Utopia* and encompassing Lewis Carroll's *Alice* novels. They are equally disarmed by the dystopian visions of films like *The Matrix,* which offers a scenario that reality itself has become a simulation: its interactive virtual-reality program leaves people recumbent in incubators, experiencing what they think is reality when in fact it is just their brain impulses reacting with the program.

The notion of a program, when viewed in relation to the potential of architecture and design, increasingly becomes part of the design task. Moreover, the overlap of building and program interactive capabilities brings to the

fore unprecedented scope to modify spatial experiences. This is one reason to be wary of formulaic 'smart' design, despite the value of GPS (global positioning systems). Once regarded as the preserve of museum exhibits or Jumbotrom advertising screens, 'smart' is a lame tag vaguely implying that all of our technical facilities can be taken care of autonomously.

As the work of Usman Haque and Jason Bruges, emerging practitioners in the field, demonstrates, interactive spaces can avoid having this form of overriding, one-dimensional, or amorphous, identity. Potentially they can promote the personalisation of the environment over the chilly 'transparent' gaze of surveillance by reacting in real time to the body as a biofeedback mechanism. This is not just a gimmick for leisure spaces, but an approach to environments where the body and mind need to attain or maintain a better harmony, for example in hospitals or while travelling – contexts Bruges and interface designer Paul Priestman are working on.

It is evident that pliable and responsive digital environments potentially constitute specific new types of structures that raise the haptic and intuitive threshold of public and private space by harnessing physical and mental responses. In the future, interactive architectural design, assisted by a wider recognition of its value as an emerging hybrid discipline, will enable the relationship between building and program to become a much more subtle and communicative process, embracing a wider, personalised set of functions, desires and experiences. ∆

Notes
1 Malcolm McCullough, *Digital Ground*, MIT Press (Cambridge, MA), 2004.
2 Staged as part of the onedotzero7 festival (www.onedotzero.com), and chaired by David Turnbull, codirector of Atopia, to whom warm thanks are due, and funded by the Arts Council of England, whose support of both the conference and feasibility research for this issue is hugely appreciated, together with the kind sponsorship of Arup Communications, and *Archis* magazine as the conference media partner. Conference speakers were Ron Arad, Ole Bouman, Jim Read/Arup Communications, Usman Haque and Josephine Pletts, Chris Allen/The Light Surgeons, Christian Grou and Tapio Snellman/Neutral, Antonino Saggio/University of Rome La Sapienza, Tobi Schneidler, Lars Spuybroek/NOX, Marcelyn Gow/servo architects, Marc Neelen/stealth, and Paul Verschure/Institute of Neuroinformatics, ETH, Zurich.

Sky Ear,

Usman Haque

Sky Ear, designed by architect and artist Usman Haque,[1] is a nonrigid 'cloud' made up of hundreds of glowing helium balloons that engage the strange hidden aural beauty of electromagnetic space. From it are suspended mobile phones, brightly coloured LEDs and electromagnetic sensors that emit different coloured lights when activated. These miniature sensor circuits (simple gaussmeters) detect levels of electromagnetic radiation at a variety of frequencies. When they are activated the sensor circuits cause the LEDs to illuminate.

Sky Ear, in the planning for three years, took its maiden voyage at Fribourg, Switzerland, in spring 2004 at the Belluard Bollwerk International Festival, prior to a formal and dramatic launch at the National Maritime Museum in Greenwich, London, in September, where this time the cloud climbed to a height of over 100 metres, watched by over 3,500 people.

Released from its ground moorings, in Switzerland, the cloud slowly floated up into the sky, the balloons enclosed in a carbon-fibre and net structure 25 metres in diameter and tethered to the ground by six cables. Once fully risen, the balloons were held aloft at a height of 60 metres. As the cloud floated upwards, it glowed and flickered as it passed through varying radio- and microwave spaces. Haque, present on the site, described its effect as 'like a glowing jellyfish sampling the electromagnetic spectrum rather like a vertical radar sweep'.

Mobile phones were the starting point of the project, as Haque is particularly interested in how they condition our use of space now that they are ubiquitous. Clearly, this was a good way to get a larger audience involved with the piece, because most people enjoy using them, whether to text friends or pursue more interactive activities, for example participation in TV's *Big Brother* reality show. 'When an audience member uses a phone during the cloud flight, they are not using it just as a remote-control device: the cloud is actually responding to the electromagnetic fields created within it by the phones,' says Haque. As visitors called into the cloud to listen to the distant electromagnetic sounds of the sky (including 'whistlers' and 'spherics' – electromagnetic phenomena, the equivalent of the Northern Lights), their mobile-phone calls changed the internal electromagnetic topography inside, these disturbances altering the glow and colour intensity of that part of the balloon cloud.

The balloons are not just buoyant floatation devices, but also diffusers for the six ultra-bright LED lights that mix with millions of colours controlled by the individual sensors inside each balloon. They can communicate with each other via infrared, creating patterns across the surface of the cloud. Feedback within the sensor network created ripples of light similar to rumbling thunder and flashes of lightning. The programme sequence is timed to the setting of the sun. At the Greenwich event, visitors on the ground as well as those on the Web were able to

> The balloons are not just buoyant floatation devices, but also diffusers for the six ultrabright LED lights that mix with millions of colours controlled by the individual sensors inside each balloon. They can communicate with each other via infrared, creating patterns across the surface of the cloud. Feedback within the sensor network created ripples of light similar to rumbling thunder and flashes of lightning.

dial up the cloud using freephone numbers and manipulate the patterns of illumination.

Haque teaches the Bartlett School of Architecture's Interactive Architecture Workshop. A trained architect, he specialises in interactive design and research, using conventional technology unconventionally to explore the ways in which people relate to each other and to their surrounding space. He designs physical environments and builds the software that brings them to life. After initially working for other architects, his subsequent experience broadened his capabilities in this area, firstly as artist-in-residence at the International Academy of Media Arts and Sciences (IAMAS) in Japan. His interactive and telecommunications works have been exhibited internationally, and with Josephine Pletts, his former partner, he was commissioned to design a global interactive tourist node by the Interaction-Ivrea technological research institute in northern Italy. They also developed interactive elements for London bus shelters, and have researched the spatial applications of smell for the Wellcome Trust, which resulted in an exhibition.

Sky Ear is supported by the Daniel Langlois Foundation for Art, Science and Technology,[2] and is Haque's most ambitious project to date: 'It stemmed from an idea I had in Japan while in the studio trying to get a

Below
Diagram by Usman Haque showing how Sky Ear's interactive elements come together. The ambient electromagnetic waves, spectators on the site and remote Web users phone up the cloud of balloons to hear the electromagnetic sounds picked up by the miniature sensor circuits. Their visual and aural responses in turn cause them to continue phoning, creating further disturbances in the electromagnetic fields inside the cloud, and as a result perpetuating changes in light and colour activity.

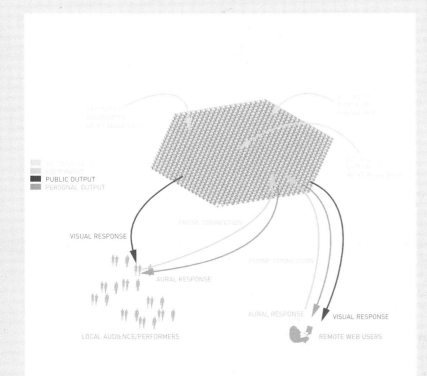

PUBLIC OUTPUT
PERSONAL OUTPUT

VISUAL RESPONSE

PHONE CONNECTION

AURAL RESPONSE

PHONE CONNECTION

LOCAL AUDIENCE/PERFORMERS

AURAL RESPONSE

VISUAL RESPONSE

REMOTE WEB USERS

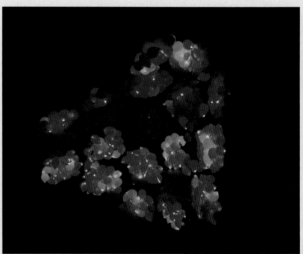

good reception on the radio and, sensing that it was similar to trying to find a good signal on my mobile, I imagined the qualities of electromagnetic space that are present everywhere.' He was originally going to make a radar grid, revealing the undulating nature of the waves.

'Electromagnetic waves exist just about everywhere in our atmosphere,' says Haque. 'The cloud will show both how a natural invisible electromagnetism pervades our environment and also how our mobile-phone calls and text messages delicately affect the new and existing electromagnetic fields.' These waves have long since existed as natural phenomena – distant storms, radiowaves emanating from distant stars, gamma rays from elements here on earth, or even electrical waves inside our own skulls. More recently, human beings have begun contributing to the situation with mobile phones, pagers, medical devices, television broadcasts, with mobiles and power lines giving cause for alarm about the health effects of electromagnetic radiation.

Haque says that electromagnetic space – also called Hertzian space by Tony Dunne, the designer and author – is physical and nonvirtual: 'It consists of a ghostly poetic ecology that exists just beyond our familiar perceptual limits,' he adds. 'The universe is the oldest radio in the world,' he says, quoting Dunne.[3] Rather than

Electromagnetic space – also called Hertzian space – is physical and nonvirtual. It consists of a ghostly poetic ecology that exists just beyond our familiar perceptual limits. The universe is the oldest radio in the world. Rather than being pervasive globally, urban locations in particular have a diverse and vibrant Hertzian culture, with mobile-phone calls overlapping text messages, combining television broadcasts with garage-door openers that interfere with radio transmissions from wireless laptops and so on.

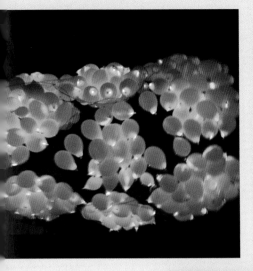

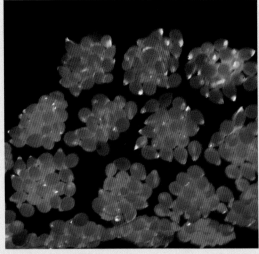

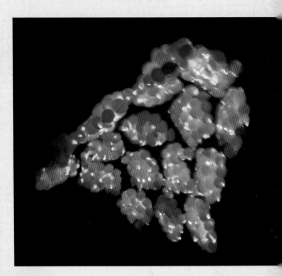

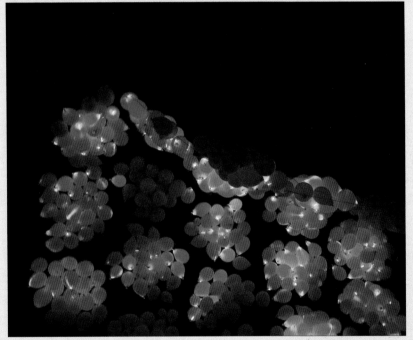

Notes
1 www.haque.co.uk.
2 www.fondation-langlois.org.
3 Tony Dunne, *Hertzian Tales*,
Royal College of Art (London),
1994.

Opposite page, top right,
and above
Sky Ear's cloud of balloons
slowly floated into the sky,
to be held at a height of 60
metres. As it floated upwards,
the cloud glowed and flickered
as it passed through varying
radio- and microwave spaces.

Right and bottom right
As visitors called into the cloud
to listen to the distant
electromagnetic sounds of the
sky, their mobile-phone calls
changed the internal
electromagnetic topography
inside, disturbances which
altered the glow and colour
intensity of that part of the
balloon cloud.

being pervasive globally, 'urban locations in
particular have a diverse and vibrant Hertzian
culture, with mobile-phone calls overlapping text
messages, combining television broadcasts with
garage-door openers that interfere with radio
transmissions from wireless laptops and so on'.
The balloons, being more than just detectors,
function as cellular automata, and Haque
envisages creating larger patterns with them
all talking to each other.

Sky Ear is a ground-breaking project because
it breaks the perceptual boundaries between
the physical and virtual by encouraging people
to become creative participants in a Hertzian
performance, allowing us to see our daily
interactions within the invisible topographies
of Hertzian space. ⌂

ICE,

Klein Dytham Architecture and Toshio Iwai

Bloomberg Headquarters

The activities of international news agency Bloomberg harvest financial data and news from innumerable global sources, and process it into a form that is understandable. Since late 2002, the firm's high-rise headquarters in Marunouchi, behind Tokyo Station, has been graced by an installation in a dedicated space on the ground floor visible from the street. The installation permits staff and visitors to process and play with data in a very tangible and experiential way. ICE – the interactive communicative experience – is a 'smart' info-lounge planted within this busy urban space, designed by architects Klein Dytham with leading Japanese interactive designer Toshio Iwai.

'Bloomberg is pretty wise to information dissemination in all its digital forms, and they were fully aware of interactive media: we pushed that to a much higher level', says Mark Dytham. Klein Dytham Architecture (KDa) and Toshio Iwai managed to secure a pretty good budget and wanted to create something unique and playful that had never before existed in this kind of working environment, but rejected the idea of either a cybercafé or, inevitably, a more isolated gallery environment. The installation is a 5 x 3.5 metre glass wall suspended from the ceiling like a large stalactite or icicle. It is also quite deep – at 10 centimetres – in order to be earthquake-proof. FTSE and NASDAQ financial data are lightly visible close up, represented as electronic ticker tape. If the stock is up the stock sign swells, and if it drops the sign shrinks below the line, like digital shadows that rise and fall.

Infrared sensors behind the surface detect the visitor's presence from 500 millimetres away –he or she does not need to touch it – and the data begins to interact with the individual's bodily movements, with the columns of numbers beginning to fluctuate. A menu

scrolls down the screen, giving the visitor four digital play options – a harp, a shadow, a wave or a volleyball. The sounds of music are instantly represented by glowing, bifurcating coloured light-forms like tree branches. The sensors convert movements and touch, converting them into optical and acoustic signals, inputs that are relayed back as vibrant, ever-changing reflective patterns, like manipulable fire, that cast giant electronic shadows.

KDa is already well known for its electronic billboards and three-dimensional hoardings-cum-architecture, but Wonderwall is one of the practice's first stabs at making an interactive game spatial. 'It just seemed a natural idea,' says Dytham. 'The context of Techno Tokyo allows these things to go forward unquestioned. Everything seems possible.' With its engaging interface, elegantly installed, ICE promotes the personalisation of space by reacting in real time to the body as a biofeedback mechanism. The wall is constantly processing information – information received virtually, and physical information about human presence – and converting the input it receives from the large number of electronic sensors behind the screen.

The installation is designed to last for between four and five years. It probably constitutes a new environmental genre, an alternative on-premises amusement arcade or *pachinko* parlour, and has already proved very popular. 'It's packed at the weekends with shoppers and kids,' adds Dytham. 'The security guards who hang out near the space like being assigned that position as they can go in and play with it – and show people how it works.' An innocent yet knowing design, ICE defies the boundaries between office interior and street, work and play, data and body. ∆

Lucy Bullivant is an architecture and design critic, author and curator of exhibitions and events. Guest-editor of this issue, she trained at the Royal College of Art, London, and has worked internationally since 1987, curating many international touring exhibitions and discussion events including: 'The Near and the Far, Fixed and in Flux' (XIX Milan Triennale, 1996, supported by the Cultural Affairs Department of the Foreign and Commonwealth Office); 'Kid Size: the Material World of Childhood', on children's environments within and beyond the Western world (Vitra Design Museum, Kunsthal Rotterdam, 1997, and international tour to 2004); 'Space Invaders: New UK Architecture', with Pedro Gadanho (the British Council); 'Experimenta' (Lisbon, 2001, and tour to Tallinn, Prague, Berlin, Los Angeles, Tokyo and Rio); the ICA's 'Spaced Out III' architectural series and 'Smart Practices in a Complex World' conference (1997); *Archis* magazine event series in London (1998–2001); '4dspace: Interactive Architecture', at the ICA; and 'Home Front: New Developments in Housing' for the Architectural Association (AA), which evolved from an issue of *Architectural Design* of the same name that she guest-edited in July/August 2003. Lucy contributes to *Domus*, *Harvard Design Magazine*, *Architectural Record*, I.D., *Archis*, *Architectural Design* and *Blueprint*, and lectures and chairs conferences internationally. *Anglo Files*, her latest book on the younger generation of UK architects, is due to be published by Thames & Hudson in spring 2005. *Responsive Environments*, a book on interactive spatial design for the V&A Contemporary book series, will be published in spring 2006.

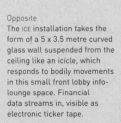

Opposite
The ICE installation takes the form of a 5 x 3.5 metre curved glass wall suspended from the ceiling like an icicle, which responds to bodily movements in this small front lobby info-lounge space. Financial data streams in, visible as electronic ticker tape.

This page
Infrared sensors behind the surface detect the visitor's presence from 500 millimetres away, and the data starts to respond to his or her movements. Glowing coloured light-forms bifurcating like tree branches appear, with synchronised music. A menu scrolls down the surface of the screen, giving the visitor four digital play options – a shadow, as shown here, a wave, a volleyball or a harp.

CYBERSPACE IS
R E A L
E S T A T E

Architecture,

Wireless, embedded communication technologies with their emphasis on human connectivity rather than the networking of place to place, no longer require the interface of bricks and mortar. **Ole Bouman** discusses the implications of this for architecture in an age in which people rather than place become the interface. He also describes how his own curatorial work has, in recent years, engaged with time-based rather than location-based technologies.

Whereas time was once considered to be the fourth dimension, it is now the first. In understanding our place in this world, it has become increasingly important to answer the question of 'when' rather than the question of 'where'. In order to comprehend what our time might be, it is essential to reverse the angle. This places emphasis on knowing or choosing your moments rather than topocentrically reeling off an address. In this age of globalisation of mind and matter, body and soul, and you and me, culture is not about being a fixed identity, but about acting, intervening, deciding, relating and transacting. Whether we like it or not, if even our genes are being negotiated by genetics and our chemical elements being transformed in nanotechnology, why should we stick to the idea that we can define 'what' and 'where'? We had better concentrate on 'how' and 'when', and start all over again from there.

So if this is true, what does it mean to architecture? For quite some time now, architects and theorists have explored the new meaning of architecture beyond the classical world-view. They have been carefully examining the way architecture could represent another cosmic order (or disorder) beyond the humanist principles and the Modernist utopias. In their Postmodern work, they blew up the meaning of architecture. But this is now old news. We are currently entering an age in which architecture has to deal not with a blow to its world-view, but with a blow to the very stuff it is made of – matter, space and human relations.

CAN ARCHITECTURE GO DIGIT-ALL?

CD-ROMIFICATION OF THE PAST IS THE PAX CYBERNETICA OF THE FUTURE

EXIT
CONDITION HUMAINE

Liquid, Gas

It is not enough for architecture to think about the temporalisation of space; it must face the spatialisation of time. Even moments need a setting – physical, digital – and this might be architecture. But to do this properly, one first needs to raise the level of time awareness among the architects. And this is exactly what this article is about.

One of the best modalities of time is connectivity. Through connectivity people synchronise, level and reassert their social relations. Still, if there is no urge, no reason, no necessity to relate to other people, there is no need for architecture. But today one could say that if there is not such an urge, there is not even humanity. In the wake of the paradigm shift described above, humanity is becoming a matrix rather than an ensemble of contingent communities. Architecture has to make the shift as well, beyond the enclosure of the sphere (to use the words of Peter Sloterdijk) and towards the spatialisation of moments in the matrix.

If you think about the way we relate to other people today; if you think about the revolution that has taken place in terms of connectivity; if you think about the dream of connectivity that underlies much of what the multimedia industries are doing these days – to connect to anybody, anywhere, any time through all the senses; and if you think about the basic agenda of design and technology today – to enhance this quality of connectivity – no one can deny the effects on the discipline of architecture. In the traditional sense of enclosing, demarcating, particularising, isolating a certain programme, architecture even becomes a bit awkward. It is in a way a hindrance to this connectivity. Architecture in the old sense becomes an embarrassment; it slows things down and moves attention away from it. At the very least one could say it marginalises from it. Architecture, in this sense, is comparable to a tariff barrier, a protectionist policy or a relic of a lost civilisation.

An example of what I have been referring to, one that makes this all sound a bit less pathetic, can be found in the common discourse or everyday rhetoric of IT, in the ubiquitous phrase 'going the last mile'. It has been used in IT speak over the last 10 years to sum up the challenge of connectivity that technology was to take in order to make the leap from the network to the house, to the location. It might be said that architecture managed to survive that age of 'going the last mile'. Today, however, we are hearing in this field of IT discourse about 'going the last yard', which means that now it's no longer about reaching the house, reaching a place, but about reaching people directly. It's about wireless, embedded technologies. It's about latent technologies. You can no longer see them. You can no longer switch them off. They reach you directly. They no longer need this venue of the house. And they don't need the interface of bricks and mortar. In fact, it is

The real revolution is to come, when 'genetech' and 'nanotech' will merge with 'infotech'. At this point, it is not just the meaning of architecture that becomes arbitrary, but its function of shelter, occupation, enclosure and material consistency.

people who are now the interface. Furthermore, it wouldn't surprise me if, within 25 years or so, people will be talking about 'going the last inch', which would mean that connectivity had become all about reaching the brain directly, no longer needing any hardware and software, but depending instead on 'orgware' and 'wetware'. The real revolution is to come, when 'genetech' and 'nanotech' will merge with 'infotech'. At this point, it is not just the meaning of architecture that becomes arbitrary, but its function of shelter, occupation, enclosure and material consistency.

So, in the context of this, it is worthwhile elaborating on some curatorial and editorial projects I have been involved in over the last 10 years that underscore this trajectory and represent flashpoints of my autobiography.

Prior to my curatorship of the first project – the 'RealSpace in QuickTimes' exhibition (the Dutch entry to the xix Milan Triennale staged in 1996) – I was working as a cultural historian and teacher. At this time I used to describe buildings as clocks, as machines that commemorate; they measure the time of history, and highlight specific events, moments or people, in history. In this sense they are about turning points in time. But these static objects of the past, of architecture as we have known it for such a long time, were also clocks in a more cyclical way. They organised our sleeping, our working, our cooking and our meal times. Ordinary buildings – potentially offices or houses – were all clocks in that respect. They had this special capacity to synchronise people and to get them together.

However, the presence within society of machines to synchronise people and, as such, the stories they tell about human culture, became problematic in the light of new emerging phenomena that raised the question of how architecture can deal with an asynchronic age

where people connect to each other in an asynchronic way, no longer being compelled to the adjacency and synchronicity imperative of human interaction, and connecting to each other just as they decide, very likely now by email for example, and using all kinds of visual interfaces that work asynchronically.

The question raised by 'RealSpace in QuickTimes' was: How can architecture adopt a technology which is in itself time-based? I tried to single out two specific aspects of the way in which digital technologies had incredible implications for architecture. The first centred on the relationship between architectural design and computer-aided design, observing the strong divergence between designers who predominantly merely adopt new technologies to facilitate the old design process, trying to make it easier, and the very few architects who have applied these new design instruments to the task of renewing and innovating through design, trying to find new forms, new strategies, new processes and new techniques. But the same polarisation applies to another important implication of these new technologies – not simply to the design of space, but to the experience of space. Again, we see an incredible number of people trying to adopt these new technologies to make environments smarter, smoother, more neutral, and capable of being monitored. However, in contrast, there are relatively few trying to use technologies facilitating smart environments to enhance people's experience, to make it more complicated but also more challenging.

So there is an opposition between this technology-driven attitude in the adoption of new media in architecture and a more user- or artist-driven attitude. In other words, there is a new technology that only produces more of the same, yet also contains the vital potential to produce a new practice, for making as well as experiencing architecture. The prediction was that this divergence of ambitions in the use of new media would be a constant pattern in the future.

The next project reversed the title of the previous one to produce 'QuickTimes in RealSpace'. Here, I tried to deal with the way in which spaces have become speeded up, quickened, and now tend towards a more liquid condition. This project was widely featured in *Archis* magazine in 1998 and became the topic of various of my public lectures. I attempted to single out four different design modes to see how each worked: thinking about how one could design with new media in terms of trying to make space more liquid, trying to enhance the experience, and trying to merge the different dimensions of the experience.

The first, most basic yet still very popular way of achieving these aims is simply to animate space. If architecture can no longer be just a dumb object or a static shelter alone, and if you want to do more, you can at least animate the surface by means of

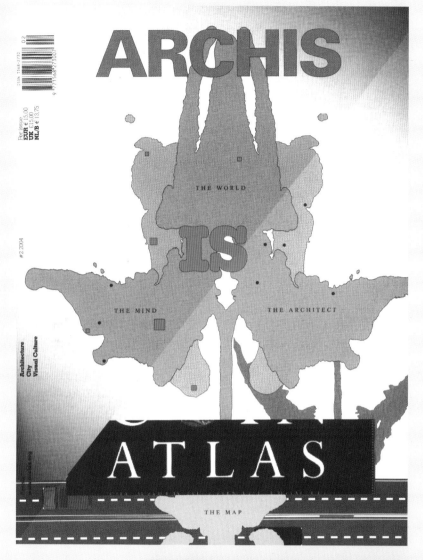

projection technology. The next stage could be to also make it interactive – and moreover make interactive spaces. Surfaces are made interactive through touchscreens, through joysticks, but also through invisible sensor technology. The third step would be to bring your environment alive, to merge different environments remotely from each other by using and inventing interfaces and overlapping the environments, for example by using the projections of one space to animate the space in the other place. The fourth stage would be to go online in order to connect remote environments, merging digital and physical environments in a single interface, accessible both in the analogue world and on the Internet.

So in this largely theoretical project, I gave a prospective overview of the consecutive steps architects make in merging physical spaces and virtual ones, overcoming the sterile dichotomy between the analogue and the digital world. On a practical level, between 2000 and 2002 I worked with architect Kas Oosterhuis on a prototype for 'trans-ports', an interactive visitor pavilion that aimed to integrate all of the aforementioned stages. Four years later, we now see a lot of surface animation, quite a few interactive environments, some interesting examples of interconnected spaces, and a small number of well-conceived fused spaces with both a real and a virtual interface. It is not difficult to predict that we will see a lot more of these kinds of projects in the near future.

The third project, 'Freeze', was an exhibition staged at the Arti et Amicitiae gallery in Amsterdam in 2000, and was more about feeling than about seeing. The main exhibit was a huge fridge: the visitor was invited to step inside its ice-lined interior, which immediately felt extremely cold yet also had the contrasting stimulus of projections on all four walls of its icy surface. Through the duration of the exhibition, the crystallisation process of the ice led to the projections gradually becoming blurred. At the beginning of the exhibition visitors could clearly see films about all kinds of digital lifestyles, but by the end, a few weeks later, there were no such projected films left, and all that remained was light play.

Inside the fridge with the door closed, you simply couldn't stay there for longer than five minutes before you were completely frozen and had to leave. This was about trying to create the sense of a 'freeze frame', a specific time span, or a personal attention span, which most of the time is extremely short. It was an attempt to enhance individual awareness of the very shortness of attention span, making the installation a medium to get rid of people as soon as possible.

More recently I have been examining the possibility of going beyond architecture as a physically structural discipline, in order to see how its very basic urge to relate people to one another can also be achieved

Main picture
Kas Oosterhuis/oosterhuis.nl and Ole Bouman, 'trans-ports' programmable visitor pavilion, 2001
Exterior of the 'trans-ports' pavilion. The data-driven supple structure had a flexible electronic skin that changed shape and content in real time.

Inset
'trans-ports' interior.

Above and right
Usman Haque, Josephine Pletts and Dr L Turin, Scents of Space, Slade School of Art, 2002
Funded by a Wellcome Trust Sciart Award, the Scents of Space interactive project demonstrated that smell can be used spatially to create fragrance collages that form soft zones and boundaries that are configurable.

Above
Dunne & Raby, FLIRT (Flexible Information and Recreation for mobile users), 1998, published by the RCA, 2000
The development of digital cellular structures by the mobile communications industry has generated a fusion between information space and urban territory. City location, the time, day and date can all begin to shape relationships to information sources. The FLIRT project, a European Commission research project under the 'IT for Mobility' theme, re-evaluated how, given the tight constraints of mobile displays and the unpredictability and transience of everyday mobility, they could work in future. It looked at the potential of location-specific information as a resource, but also as a means of social interaction and play. Dunne & Raby tailored their map, a cellular city model deemed by Helsinki Telephone Corporation to be a realistic representation of the mobile network in the city, to reflect the experiences of cellular space in public space and to serve as a tool to work through, and test out, ideas about location-based services.

through means other than constructing. Here, architecture becomes even more unstable than liquid – perhaps more like a gas. If human behaviour and interaction is no longer framed by place, but is a matter of making strategic decisions and experiencing moments at remote and asynchronically related sites, and if this very remoteness and asynchronic character of our lives can be designed as an interface, then architecture will lose its character as a consistent and integrated form of cultural communication, and will become more like a chemical process of loose particles. For some, this might be a kind of sacrilege, because if you think about 10,000 years of architectural history, and 10,000 years spent creating objects and assembling constructional parts, how could you ever believe that we are entering an era where this is merely a side effect of the way people relate to each other in a new way?

What I'm talking about represents the very early beginning of a new practice. There are a number of examples of this in this publication. In the work of Pletts Haque, such a new way of thinking operates through the dimension of smell, and the way we can relate to each other

not just through vision, but also through aromatic responses. In the work of Anthony Dunne and Fiona Raby, relations are established within the electromagnetic dimension. Theirs are projects that rely on pervasive computing, that no longer need buildings to mediate between people, but which rely on a much more ephemeral, much more subtle interface design. These architects and designers are the pioneers, though I sometimes wonder whether they fully realise which of civilisation's new thresholds they are the pioneers of, and if they really want this identity, because if this development unfolds to its logical conclusion and architecture really becomes a gas, then there is little chance that the early adopters and initial contributors will be acknowledged for this. Entropy has no authors. But that's another story.

Since 1996 I have been directing *Archis*, a magazine that has chosen to deal with the kinds of new realities described above. How do you cover such a new world that is more about time than space? How can you invent a form of journalism, a critical discourse or a reflexivity that is no longer about buildings that are used as clocks, but is about time, which of course we are spatialising all the time. I believe that we can no longer rely on a print medium that takes the physical form of a horizontal landscape, as so much of our

For a long time architecture was thought of as a solid reality and entity: buildings, objects, matter, place, and a set of geometric relationships. But recently, architects have begun to understand their products as liquid, animating their bodies, hypersurfacing their walls, crossbreeding different locations, experimenting with new geometries. And this is only the beginning.

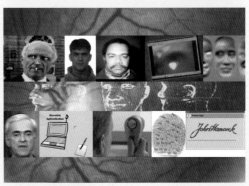

architectural media still do. Travelling through the pages of the magazine, one encounters different contributions, pictures, topics, just like scanning a landscape. There are pictures of interesting projects, boring projects. The process is not just a vertical one – going through a discourse or trying to see how the vertical layout is done in 1-D or 2-D. It's also about 3-D, about creating a space itself, and I believe that you can no longer reflect upon this new practice of architecture by using the old media. You need to spatialise the medium, which to begin with can be achieved via the creation of action pages, event spaces within the magazine that trigger learning by acting and doing – it is full of these moments. To facilitate these, all the pages are perforated, ready for action. So this is 4-D publishing, hopefully anticipating a whole new chapter of further intellectual research and development.

For a long time architecture was thought of as a solid reality and entity: buildings, objects, matter, place, and a set of geometric relationships. But recently, architects have begun to understand their products as liquid, animating their bodies, hypersurfacing their walls, crossbreeding different locations, experimenting with new geometries. And this is only the beginning. We will see more and more architects realising spatialised moments, through staging narratives, through event designing, working with effects and emotions. Of course there will be a need for shelter, so there will be a practice of making sheds. But, to use the famous dichotomy of Robert Venturi, the decoration will not be the facade. Things will be communicated, but not to glorify any past, nor to embrace any future. Things will be told in flashes, by flashes, through flashes. Architecture will still be about highlighting. But this time it is to get people high, to get 'em lite. ⏃

Above
Dunne & Raby, FLIRT (Flexible Information and Recreation for mobile users), 1998
Computer-generated model showing radio propagation in relation to an urban environment. In researching FLIRT, Dunne & Raby determined that although radio signals are invisible, they have a physical relationship to mass. In a similar way to light, the mass of a building reduces signal strength and creates radio 'shadows'. The more dense the built-up area, the more antennae are needed to ensure good coverage.

Right
'Freeze' exhibition, Arti et Amicitiae gallery, Amsterdam, April 2000
Curated by Ole Bouman, the exhibition included a huge fridge as its main exhibit. Inside, videos of digital lifestyle activities and body scans were projected onto the the icy walls. Exhibition design by Eden (René van Raalte and Ronald van der Meijs), audiovisuals by Harold Houdijk.

Ole Bouman is an internationally known critic, author, designer and curator based in Amsterdam. He is editor-in-chief of *Archis* magazine and director of the Archis RSPV Events, as well as the author of several books including *The Invisible in Architecture* (1994), *RealSpace in QuickTimes: Architecture and Digitization* (also the title of the exhibition he curated for the XIX Triennale di Milano at the NAi, 1996), and *The Battle for Time* (2003). Other exhibitions he has curated include 'Egotecture' (Boijmans van Beuningen Museum, Rotterdam, 1997) and 'Freeze' (Arti et Amicitiae, Amsterdam, 2000). He also lectures internationally.

Interactivity at the Centre of Avant-Garde Architectural Research

The onset of digital technologies is often cited as the determining force behind the recent paradigm shift in architecture. Here, **Antonino Saggio** makes the case for interactivity. He argues that it is interactivity rather than hardware or software that has been the essential catalyst, providing the fundamental precepts underlying contemporary communications and bringing with it a new configuring of relationships in which the subject takes centre stage and shifts the object to the periphery.

How and why is the concept of interactivity currently so central to architectural research in this period of history? Firstly, interactivity is now the catalysing element of architectural research and development activity because it is within this that the contemporary communication system, based on the possibility of creating metaphors and so of firstly navigating and then building hypertextual systems, resides. Secondly, interactivity places at its centre the subject (variability, reconfigurability, personalisation) instead of the absolute nature of the object (serialisation, standardisation, duplication). Thirdly, interactivity incorporates the fundamental feature of computer systems, namely the possibility of creating

interconnected, changeable models of information that can be constantly reconfigured. And lastly, interactivity plays, in structural terms, with time, and indicates an idea of continuous 'spatial reconfiguration' that changes the borders of both time and space that until now have been consolidated.[1]

Hypertexts and the Creation of Metaphors: Interactivity Within the World of Communications

Many of us will still remember the ways in which architecture used to be taught us. For a long time, the key word was objectivity. We had always to demonstrate analytically the relationship between a cause and a specific solution; good architecture sprang from this association. However, this way of thinking has now gone out of fashion, together with the great industrial model. Today, narration holds pride of place. Consequently, what comes first is the story to be told, and it is only after and within this narrative that the project develops. There are examples of this in front of us all.

We must also add a second factor to this narrative component, and it is here that interactivity comes into play. More and more, contemporary communication is also metaphorical. Metaphor replaces a unidirectional cause–effect reasoning with pluridimensionality and the discontinuity of rhetorical figures. Instead of advances being made in a linear manner, they are made by hops and jumps.

But is not hypertext the communicative setting of these jumps? With HTML (hypertext mark-up language), its links and the Internet, is hypertext not an inalienable part of our way of thinking today?

The most fitting definition of hypertextual systems is that of being themselves settings in which metaphors are created. The challenge in this sector lies not only in creating predefined metaphors (for example, an artist's production exhibited in his virtual studio), but also that of being able to have 'mobile metaphors' that can be reconfigured each time by the user. An ever-growing number of systems is able to create actual metaphors that can be personalised (consider, for example, the creation of scenarios that can be played or visited through the use of artificial intelligence techniques, or searches in databases that can be personalised, or virtual simulations).

By this we mean that interactivity thrusts the sphere of contemporary communication towards a more complex level: metaphors and images that are already defined begin to be replaced with the idea that we can ourselves create our own metaphors. This is the great challenge of the world of hypertextual communication. It is an open battle, one that is also political and social, and that implicates the development of an increasingly mature critical sense. When I teach, from the outset I ask all my students to create and publish their own web pages: this is no coincidence.

Interactivity and the Computer World

Information technology is the underlying 'mental landscape' of today's architecture. By mental landscape I mean that architectural research (since the outset) prefigures the ideal context in which it is located. Architecture prefigures this mental landscape by supporting some elements already present in reality, developing other elements and, above all, incorporating scientific or symbolic models that have succeeded each other over time. That is, architecture transforms these models into specific spatial interpretations.

Information technology is based on the characteristic of building 'mobile' and 'interconnected' models of information. These are movable models because they change a datum, or because by changing a relationship they modify the results. This intrinsically dynamic, intrinsically interconnected mental landscape re-creates reality in the form of mathematical relationships and processes. Interactivity in this context results in architecture being constantly modifiable and forming a sensitive setting in constant transformation – a setting that can also react with, and adapt to, a shift in users' desires through the creation of scenarios that can be explored as though they were hypertexts.

Just as Renaissance architecture transformed itself into something 'perspective-able', and just as Functionalist architecture completely restructured itself to become 'industry-able' (and I do not mean 'only' an architecture that wants to reveal the objective, serial, abstract, mechanical essence of the industrialised world), so today's architecture is struggling to be 'information-able': it is struggling to incorporate within itself the dynamic, interconnected and, above all, interactive essence of the IT-based paradigm.

Interactivity and Time

Now we come to the last set of considerations, which is in some sense the most complex.

Information technology is based on the characteristic of building 'mobile' and 'interconnected' models of information. These are movable models because they change a datum, or because by changing a relationship they modify the results. This intrinsically dynamic, intrinsically interconnected mental landscape re-creates reality in the form of mathematical relationships and processes. Interactivity in this context results in architecture being constantly modifiable and forming a sensitive setting in constant transformation.

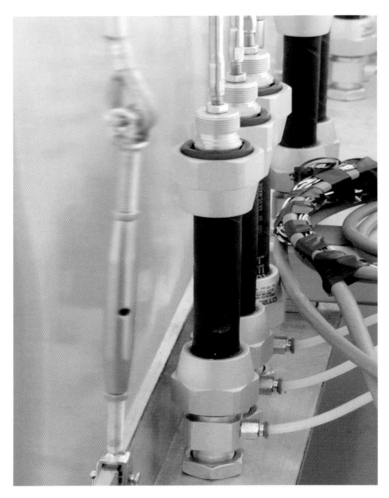

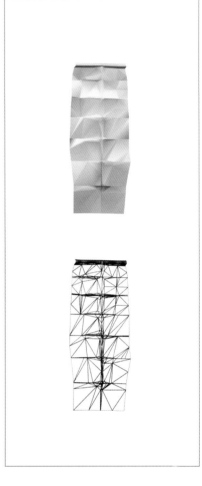

Interactivity is associated with time, which as Einstein himself wrote, is the only way to say something sensible about space. Let us recall some fundamental concepts. In the first place, space is not an objective reality (as we often believe), but is perceived culturally, historically and scientifically in very different ways. If we use time as a system for understanding space, we discover something that is highly effective. The jump rule prevails from one reference system to the other; it is the same jump that underlies hypertextual systems. (If I live in and know only a two-dimensional system – imagine a curved sheet of paper – in order to go from one point to another, I follow a route equal to T. Even if I curve the surface greatly, T still remains the same length. But if I look at this curved sheet from a three-dimensional world, I immediately note that A and B can be linked not only by segment T, but also by a far shorter spatial vector, 't', which travels, or rather jumps, through three-dimensional space.)

Interactivity in buildings can mean not only varying configurations and spaces according to changes in wishes or external input (as we have just seen), but also creating different systems of spatio-temporal reference. If an interactive system modifying architecture is linked to Internet-based navigational systems, the effect of the jump can pervade the whole of architecture: a jump from one spatial configuration to another, a jump between different information systems and, finally, a jump between different temporal states.

Associated with window interface systems, real-time navigation systems, remote depiction systems with naturally interactive, hologram-based systems (a brief step forward that will shortly be made), the great world of the Internet can form an incredible 'thickener' and multiplier of spaces and times. We can have windows open at the same time on worlds far distant from each other, and literally jump from one to the other: live in them, try out accelerating or moving spaces, show and be shown, and all this in real time and in a continuous jump from one world to the other. The Internet is a necessary instrument for architecture in this stage of research, not only because of its pragmatic aspects, but also for its cognitive ones. As we learn more, we understand how a fundamental formulation takes effect through Internet and interactivity: from a lower system, we can have the projection of a higher level. This formulation means that it is possible, although

The interactivity incorporated within the physical nature of buildings means working at a new level of architectural complexity. But the greatest challenge of all is not scientific, nor technological. And neither is it even functional. No, the true challenge is, as always, of an aesthetic nature.

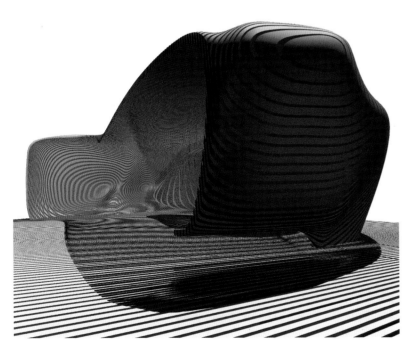

physically located within fixed three-dimensional spatiotemporal limits, to have ideas about a space with more dimensions than our own, and to use, imagine and, to some extent, understand it; even to design this multidimensional space.

At this point, I hope that it is now clear how three key questions can be traversed by the concept of interactivity. First of all, through the relationship with the world of contemporary communication and a greater subjectivity of choices (and both these components have an obvious implication with regard to the critical and political development of singularity). Moreover, interactivity is a central factor in the mental landscape of the new architectural research (through the absorption of the dynamic models of information technology). Finally, interactivity makes it possible to start to design and imagine spaces and architecture that develop in not just three dimensions, but which project upon themselves the possibility of further dimensions through the process of jumping and discontinuity.

The interactivity incorporated within the physical nature of buildings means working at a new level of architectural complexity. But the greatest challenge of all is not scientific (creating increasingly mature mathematical models), nor technological (creating the physical and electronic systems to enable levels of interactivity and sensibility in buildings and settings). And neither is it even functional (understanding how to make interactivity an element of research in the 'crises' and difficulties of contemporary society, rather than just a game in the homes of the super-rich). No, the true challenge is, as always, of an aesthetic nature. Searching for an aesthetic (that is, a way of seeing, interpreting and building the world of architecture) that is deeply and necessarily interactive. It is here that the role of the catalyst comes back into the picture.

Interactivity is the chemical reagent, the catalyst of all these components. It has, simultaneously, an ethical and a political component, and a technical and a technological one, and it also has a fundamental aesthetic component because it requires a revolution in sensing that pushes for a new awareness of

This page and opposite
dECOi, Bankside Paramorph, London, 2002
An extension to a tower-top apartment next to the Tate Modern in London, Bankside Paramorph is an exercise in 'parametric propensity', exploring the generative capacity of the variable relational modelling made possible with digital technologies.

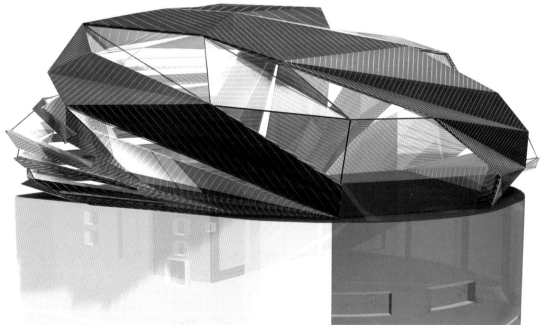

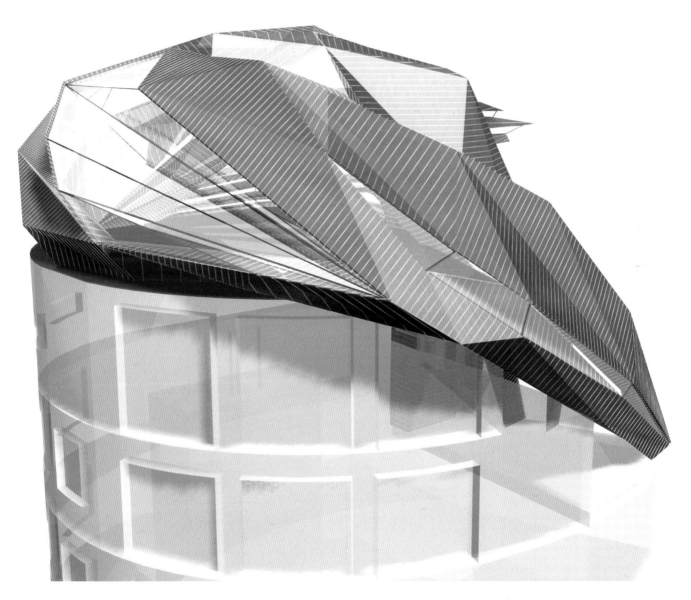

contemporariness. Looking in an extremely summary manner at the change in the picture of contemporary architecture, we can say that if the formula for the Modern Movement was rightly *Neue Sachlichkeit* (New objectivity), the formula for today cannot be other than New Subjectivity. And it is interactivity that is the key to this new subjectivity.

Transparency used to be the aesthetic, and ethics the reason and technique of a world that wanted rationally to tackle an advance in civilisation in terms of quality of life for the great masses of industrial workers. Today, by contrast,

interactivity constitutes a point of aggregation for present-day considerations about an architecture that, having gone beyond the objectivity of needs, can now tackle within its own modifications the subjectivity the desires of today's men and women. ⊅

Note
1 These points are developed extensively in the volumes of *The IT Revolution in Architecture* series, a major editorial project I initiated in 1998, published by Birkhäuser, Testo & Immagine (Italian) and Prominence (Chinese).

Antonino Saggio is professor of architecture at the University of Rome La Sapienza, an architect and planner, and the founder and editor of the book series *The IT Revolution in Architecture*, which now numbers 25 titles. He is the author of several books, including publications on Giuseppe Terragni, Peter Eisenman and Frank Gehry, and co-founded the magazine *Il Progetto*. He lectures internationally, and his website (www.citicord.uniroma1.it/saggio/) is a point of reference in architectural culture in Italy and internationally.

Building as Interface

Or, What Architects Can Learn From Interaction Designers

Walter Aprile and **Stefano Mirti** have been engaged as designers, researchers and teachers at Interaction-Ivrea, a technological research institute in northern Italy, since it was established by Telecom Italia and Olivetti in 2001. Here, the two reflect on the series of experiments they have undertaken at the intersection of interactive technology and architecture, analysing their own working systems and the means by which they have chosen to pursue interdisciplinary dialogue.

Probably the best contribution Interaction-Ivrea can make to contemporary architecture and design discourses is to define what it does. Interaction-Ivrea is not a traditional academic institution, nor is it a research centre: it borrows certain elements from both, and adds the electrifying tension and risk of evolving real-world projects. Teaching generates professional opportunities, as the people and companies who take part in our courses and workshops develop the ideas that emerge there and turn them into real projects. Examples of this are our work with the Illy coffee brand, the Aquafan water amusement park and Prada. At the same time, the impact and benefits of such projects are filtered back into teaching: Interaction-Ivrea is a place where 'learning by doing' is a fact, not a worn-out motto.

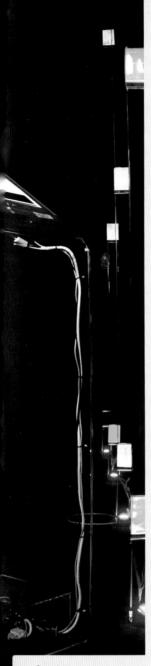

Opposite
Interaction-Ivrea with Cliostraat, Grace Under Pressure, Venice Biennale, 2002
The visitor entered a darkened space with six information touch screens. As the individual browsed the local website, getting information about DARC (the Direzione Generale per l'Architettura e l'Arte Contemporanee of the Italian Ministry of Culture), his or her activities influenced the blinking of the suspended electroluminescent slides around him or her. The Ivrea team designed the website, the physical space, all the technological support and the terminals: one issue of interaction design is that you often have to do everything yourself, as it can be difficult to give specifications clear enough for a contractor. Interaction-Ivrea: Walter Aprile, Massimo Banzi, Franziska Huebler, Stefano Mirti, Chris Noessel, Sergio Paolantonio, Jeremy Tai Abbett Cliostraat: Matteo Pastore and Luca Poncellini.

The institute is an odd mixture of designers, technologists, computer scientists and researchers, some with business-oriented minds. It is an independent, nonprofit organisation[1] located midway between Mont Blanc and Turin that offers a two-year masters programme in interaction design. Above we stressed the importance of learning by doing; however, we would now like to contradict ourselves immediately by instead theorising about what we consider to be the necessary conditions for a productive meeting between high tech/new media and architecture.

Firstly, processes and tools interest us more than aesthetics and iconic statements. Nonetheless, we acknowledge the importance and relevance of aesthetics. But we must not forget that technology and technologists have their own concept of aesthetics and appropriate form. The designer is not the only character in play.

We want to avoid pyramid structures where the architect/designer/pharaoh is on top and technologists (software, hardware, electronic) drag multi-tonne blocks through the landscape. Our vision is a horizontal circle with characters from different disciplines talking to each other, in which there are no grease monkeys, but where all are partners working together. This interdisciplinary dialogue is the most important (and difficult) element of the whole process.

The best way to produce a working structure is to iterate rough prototypes methodically. Ideate, make a cardboard mock-up, do it again, adapt, add some electronics, motherboards, Styrofoam, accept mistakes, try again, another time. When the project is over, track carefully all the mistakes and look for an opportunity to do the same project again, only better.[2]

We follow the 'form follows fiction' approach, rather than 'function follows form'. First and foremost, projects must tell a good, believable story in which the listener can find a place for him- or herself.

Though Italian, we love to indulge in the great British tradition of science and social fiction. We are not referring so much to HG Wells or JG Ballard, but to the work that challenges us on a more fundamental level, for example Thomas Moore's *Utopia*, Swift's *Gulliver's Travels*, Lewis Carroll's *Alice* novels, Edwin Abbott's *Flatland*, and The Who's *Tommy*. Though we started with Utopia, we often find Dystopia even more capturing: the work of Orwell, Terry Gilliam's *Brazil*, Stanley Kubrick's *A Clockwork Orange*. But where does architecture come in?

At the frontier of architecture there cannot be clearly expressed objective necessities: no user, no client nor committee can really say they need a mediatheque as a metaphor of information flow, since nobody knows exactly what a mediatheque might be. No client will state a requirement for a facade of iris-like glass and metal components that react to the sun. A mediatheque, a reactive facade, tells and embodies stories, and these stories are our core business.[3]

In the stories we try to tell, we generally start from the question 'What if?' This is the same question posed by science-fiction stories, by Archigram's 'What if a building could walk?' or Cedric Price's 'What if a building could be constantly generated and regenerated?'

What we find interesting in the field of interactive design now comes from this rich lode of thought: we refer to the outstanding books by Tony Dunne and Fiona Raby. Or to young designers such as Elio Caccavale ('What if we had to live with our own genetically compatible pig?'), Crispin Jones ('What if our cellphone could inflict physical pain on us?') and Noam Toram ('What if your furniture could feed you subliminal messages?').

It is clear that our references are the Londoncentric world Gillian Crampton Smith (our director at Interaction-Ivrea) made us discover: they show us how to design by building intriguing and unexpected scenarios. From this point of view, the piece or the environment we design is a part of the scenario. Our work for the Venice Biennale was based on 'What if you could walk inside a screen?' However, Eyal Fried and Luther Thie[4] posed a smarter question: 'What if brain fingerprinting became as easy as traditional fingerprinting?' – What products would result? Where would it surface first? Probably in an airport, as part of the security process. What would it feel like?

Once we have a story that can fascinate the people around us, we can start talking about the budget and the regulations and the form. We need to fascinate the people not because we like to bask in affection, but rather because we usually require a huge amount of support and supplies that cannot be obtained by other means.

Over the last three years we have made a series of experiments centred on the intersection of interactive technologies and architecture. The technologies involved – sensing, computation and display – are in a state of rapid flux. While the evolution of basic technologies and materials might be more or less predictable, the standards and applied technologies undergo frequent change. It is very easy for certain specific technologies or aesthetics (for example, green LEDS) to quickly look 'old'. Incorporating these fleeting elements of practice into buildings whose life span extends across decades would make us uncomfortable.

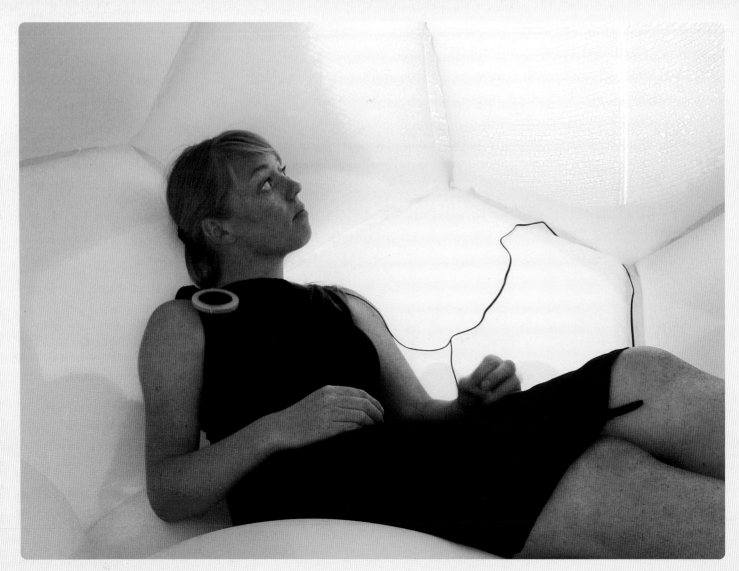

Above
Line Ulrika Christianssen, Re-Lounge, thesis project at Interaction-Ivrea, 2003
The traveller in transit at international airports can enjoy private time in a personalised environment that conforms to his or her desires with customised music and lighting. A gentle vibration warns travellers that it is almost time for boarding. The project uses as a starting point Chillout Room designed by David Sevoir, and kindly supplied by roominteriorproducts.

Rapidly changing technologies call for a prototype-based approach, perhaps closer to the world of product design than to traditional architecture.

Change means, nay, guarantees, obsolescence. One could try to delay obsolescence by using the latest and greatest technologies, for example OLEDs (organic light emitting diodes) as light sources. But on the other hand, we know that getting technology to work for some time, or even to work at all, is still the main challenge. So to increase this challenge by using still-exotic technology is perhaps not so wise.

Our guideline so far has been to use off-the-shelf parts as much as possible, and concentrate on temporary structures and installations that do not have the opportunity to get old. This allows us to make mistakes, and to learn from them. We are very clear that our work so far has been a form of practice, training and experimenting. We are not yet at the Olympics.[5]

Our first experiment was Grace Under Pressure, an interactive environment for DARC, the Direzione Generale per l'Architettura e l'Arte Contemporanee of the Italian Ministry of Culture. DARC commissioned us[6] to embed a set of significant institutional memories into a neutral space. The memories took the form of videos and images provided primarily by DARC.

We defined the space with a grid of pulsating information objects, controlled by finite state automata[7] that reacted to the users' actions. The trails of browsing produced constellations of blinking lights in the black boundless space of the room, in Biennale Gardens in Venice, as the perceptual qualities of colour and blink rate became modified by the accumulated behaviour of visitors. In this first experiment, the software and the interaction completely defined a space that, without the interactive elements, would have been neither accessible nor meaningful; in a sense the architecture of the space was software.

In Grace Under Pressure we added behaviour to a space that was blank but given. The first image in this article demonstrates what we mean when we refer to the need for aesthetic qualities that can speak to the designer as well as to the technologist.

The following series of experiments was inspired by reflecting on the thesis work of Shyama Duriseti (traditional Indian space wisdom and new media) and Line Ulrika Christianssen[8] (traveller's bubble for airport lounges). Subsequent work in the Europan 7 architecture competition tried to address the question of prototyping space itself. The technology that made most sense to us in this context was inflatables.[9] We discovered that the cheapest kind of white nylon material works quite well as a projection and back-projection screen. Our first prototype – an experimental housing system – taught us[10] many things about air circulation, solar gain, and a number of apparently minor technical issues. Quite separately from these technical aspects, we determined another interesting requirement of inflatables: you cannot do them by yourself. From the smallest size upwards, this technology requires collaboration for setup, operation and dismantling, and more so if they are interactive. This matched perfectly with the accent on collaboration that runs through the Interaction-Ivrea curriculum.

In our next exercise with inflatables we employed them as the medium for the first term of teaching, christening them CICCIO (Curiously Inflatable Computer Controlled Interactive Objects) and giving them to the class together with a microcontroller development kit. Two teams of students used them in distinct and unexpected ways. Giovanni Cannata and Anurag Sehgal designed Creative Collisions, an object that secreted all its machinery inside the CICCIO and used the external skin of the inflatable to present the visitor with an interactive surface that reacts to thrown objects with graphics and sound. Meanwhile, the Audiograffiti team (Andreea Chelaru, Ben Dove, Noel Perlas and

Thomas Stovicek) defined a white environment in which voices and sounds could be recorded and left for a while, like idle writing on a sandy shore, to be heard by successive visitors.

Another CICCIO project, done with the fundamental collaboration of Daniele Mancini, took the concept to INARCH (the Instituto Nazionale di Architettura in Rome), for a workshop within the digital architecture course[11] organised by professor and architectural critic Maria Luisa Palumbo. Here, the inflatable environment met with a radio frequency identification (RFID)[12] reactive system that we had previously designed for another context. The visitor would hold a bottle of wine, a dish of cookies, or a piece of chocolate up to a reader, and a short student-produced video segment would be projected through a window cut in the inflatable skin. The idea was carried out by Daniele Mancini as a thesis project, and presented at the end of the year show. On this occasion, the system powered a portable museum about the tourist experience in Rome. The visitor would hold up to the reader common tourist knickknacks, and the system would present a segment of video that either related the story of the object, or freely associated with fragments of classic movies about Rome. The concept driving the portable museum was that the highly mobile curator would wander around shooting video, collecting objects and presenting daily builds of his museum-in-progress.

We believe that this sequence of experiments and iterations highlights the value of choosing one theme and sticking to it. In this case, we stuck to the theme of inflatables, gradually making them more complex and interactive. While there were many small technical findings, the main lesson was a metalesson: experimental technology cannot be right first go. Iteration is required to move forward. In this, all of our projects are partial successes because we learned something, and partial failures because, in attempting to add new elements, we were not fully prepared for them. Looking at them in retrospect, we realise how much we have learned that we could not have learned from books. With regard to inflatables, for example, we learned that sphere-shaped inflatables are expensive to make, and that inflatables smaller than a minivan collapse too rapidly when visitors enter and exit.

After experimenting with the inflatable on the ground, we decided to branch into helium balloons for a number of experiments at the launch party of *Cluster* magazine, held at the Mole Antonelliana in Turin. Students experimented with connecting different environments through projections on flying screens. The visitor entered the building, saw a strange but inviting panel and put his or her head into a cutout. A camera discreetly took a picture of the visitor's face, and stored it on disk. The image was then put into a loop and projected in the main hall of the Mole, an

Below
Interaction-Ivrea, Experimental housing system, Europan 7 architecture competition, 2003
Russian doll-like inflatables proposed a light and cheap solution to the problem of housing on a riverside site in Pescara, Italy. When a living space is needed, the inflatable unit would be placed on a concrete pad, connected to services and inflated in a matter of minutes. We preferred building a 1:1 model to making renderings. This was our first experiment with inflatable structures, at the time still without interactive elements.

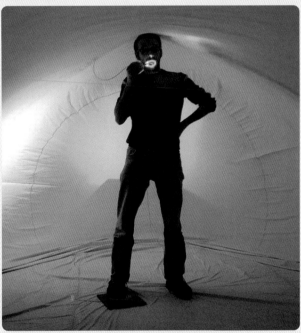

Above
Giovanni Cannata and Anurag Sehgal, Creative Collisions, and Jennifer Bove, Simone Pia and Nathan Waterhouse, Collabolla, first-year project, 2003
Creative Collisions (to the right) was designed to test a very engaging mode of interaction: the users threw objects at a CICCIO, and the surface reacted with graphics and sounds. Collabolla (in the centre) proposed a new way of interacting with classic video games by playing with your whole body and forcing the user to collaborate with a fellow player.

Right
Andreea Chelaru, Ben Dove, Noel Perlas, Thomas Stovicek, Audiograffiti, first-year project, 2003
A white environment where voices and sounds could be recorded and left, like traces on the sand, for future visitors. Sounds echoed and faded over time; the microphones were activated by the visitor stepping on a button on the floor.

enormous vaulted space that just begs to be invaded. As the visitor arrived in the hall, he or she saw his or her surprised face everywhere, projected on the CICCIOs and on helium-balloon screens flying above the party crowd. The final aesthetic result was quite crude; however, the process was smooth. What we aimed for here, in keeping with the party context, was surprise and delight, and it again confirmed how much people love seeing their own image in a delayed mirror. This event started a relationship with *Cluster* magazine that resulted in Interaction-Ivrea curating the special-interest section of the magazine's third issue on interaction, which was then distributed at the Salone del Mobile 2004.

Another important element of our work is that although at Interaction-Ivrea there is indeed a difference between students and faculty, this difference is not necessarily reflected in the project hierarchy. Different projects demand different leaderships: for example, the event at the Mole Antonelliana was built around the Face to Face to Face interactive game designed by Giorgio Olivero, at the time still a student.

Giorgio Olivero with Peggy Thoeny developed the environment research direction for the Tableportation thesis project. Tableportation exploited the ambiguous private/public status of the surface of a table in a club, and augmented it with a new expressive layer, linking it with other tables to form a shared projected environment. The additional layer used discreet touch sensors, embedded LEDs and software to turn the table top into a drawing surface, thus adding new functions and meanings to a well-

known object. Developing the project within an acceptable budget required support from Osram. The project prompted us to think lucidly in terms of promoting interactive projects to companies. Designers are prone to living in a hermetic world inhabited by themselves, the client and a number of suppliers. In the world of new technologies, suppliers must be turned into partners – an old business-school chestnut that means that your success must contain a portion of success for them too.

As they grow, projects change in nature and refocus their topic. For example, Dario Buzzini (then a student), together with Massimo Banzi (professor of physical computing), developed a project called Not So White

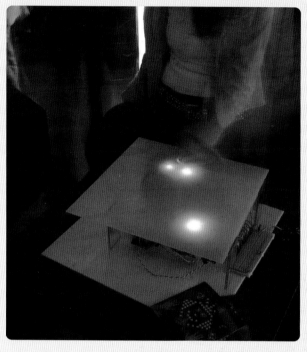

Walls with the idea of reinventing wallpaper by imbuing it with interactive qualities. The most remarkable element of this interactive wallpaper has been the development of a display that uses heat-sensitive ink and a resistor matrix to present large-scale pixilated images. These images change slowly, with a refresh rate that can be measured in seconds, and are made of reflected light, just like traditional writing or painting on paper. We consider this to be a signal example of the appropriate use of technology, since such an effect would not be obtainable via other means (such as projections, LEDs or video walls), and because it develops its own poetic qualities of slow and subliminal change. What is perhaps more important is that this display does not add more boxes to our cluttered living landscapes; when it is powered off, it is just a plain wall with no visible elements of technology.

The project has gone through four iterations and is now entering the commercial stage.[13] Developing an academic project into one of commercial-level feasibility is another step in complexity that shines a particularly strong light on yet another requirement for an interaction designer: social competence.[14] But, as Joachim Sauter[15] reminded us: 'Design is easy. Social competence is the most difficult thing to teach.'

Interactive wallpaper uses high technology in a peculiar way; the computer disappears as a visible presence – we just get its effect – and technology is used in a discreet and effective way. There are three reasons for considering discreetness and effectiveness as general conditions of success for the use of technology in design. The first is historical: mechanical aesthetics was already slightly ridiculous 50 years ago. The Dymaxion house and vehicle, or Le Corbusier's Voiture Maximum, are quaint examples not to be taken as models. Our favourite Le Corbusier buildings are the Indian ones, because they are timeless. Perhaps because we know machines, we know that there is no ghost (or spirit) inside them – not even in digital machines.

The second reason is practical: technology ages, and its ostentation has called attention to its unsightly rapid ageing. The Eames used the high technology of their time for process reasons, to obtain a shape, a product, a value – not because they suffered from technological aesthetics. As much as we love the Eames' products, we do not completely get the way Piano and Rogers used technology for the Centre Pompidou. If we enter a Romanic church, our heart rate picks up. A Baroque church leaves us a little colder. Technobaroque, more so.

In a sense, the problem of making technology visible or invisible is a false one. The real problem is that it should not be an ostentation. To show off technology per se is evidence of a cargo cult[16] mindset that warps the reasoning along these lines: if the computer is cutting edge, and it can generate blobby shapes on high-end plasma screens, I will design a building that is blobby and covered with plasma screens, and therefore I will be cutting edge. The engineer who designs the plasma screens is a hero; the architect who uses them along the lines we have mentioned is a member of a cargo cult.

A third reason is that we believe technology is for use, not for show: it cannot be a carrier of aesthetic values because its values are based on internal consistency and physical constraints. To overload it with aesthetics breaks its back.[17]

Chairman Mao used to remind us of the relationship between the finger pointing to the moon and the moon itself. As he reminds us, we don't want to call attention to the humble finger, but to the moon. If, then, people keep staring at fingers, it is their problem.

Our largest-scale public experiment so far has been the 'Interactive Body Snatchers' exhibition, held at the Milan Triennale, in the context of the Salone del Mobile 2004.[18] Here, we presented 20 projects by students, faculty and designers we frequently work with. Everything we were showing carried, as it were, a large 'Please, Do Touch' sign, and in fact the room made very

little sense without people in action. The materials used were basic and affordable: industrial rubber flooring, backstage scaffolding, no carpeting. We didn't want to show fancy results; we wanted to show the real features of our designs. The process became the aesthetic quality. As a general strategy, we say that if, for the time being, we are not able to come up with polished results, then we show rough prototypes.[19] The school was able to do most of the lighting via combination lamps/information panels, which allowed us to concentrate our energies on guaranteeing that everything we showed was interactive and operational for five full days.

The 'Interactive Body Snatchers' show has been described as friendly, engaging, rough and certainly different from the typical high-tech show-off exhibition. It worked only because, before it, we had made two smaller-scale tests, one at the institute and one in the Bu.net Internet café in Turin. The show stated clearly what we think of technology: it is something to be grabbed, used and flexed, but certainly not to be revered or admired for itself. The pieces we exhibited are evidence of a constant process of experimental negotiation between budget, aesthetic values and desire. But the key element of the show was that we were harnessing emotion, not technology.

Creative Collisions and Collabolla[20] were first shown at the Salone del Mobile and then reworked as the basis for performance pieces presented in the Media House section of Fabbrica Europa, a month-long international performance arts festival held annually in Florence. Interactive spaces were also explored in a thesis project by Tarun Jung Rawat,[21] who developed fragments of interaction for a possible museum of writing and computing techniques.

Finally, at the institute's end-of-year party, we used the facade of Talponia, our student residence, for a number of partially interactive projections. People could send text SMSs and their texts were projected on the curved-glass wall. This was at the beginning of the summer, the end of our year-long efforts. To be honest,[22] even though the image was nice, almost nothing worked properly. We set some design goals and we failed on most of them.

So was it a disaster? Not at all – as long as we acknowledge our failures, understand them and see ways around them. We did our postmortem and now we know what to fix. In this field, being humble is useful. But being honest is a condition of survival.

Above
Dario Buzzini, Not So White Walls, thesis project, 2004
The last in a series of prototypes on rethinking the wallpaper concept, this large-scale environmental display used a thin array of resistors to form an image by gently heating cloth dyed with heat-sensitive ink. When turned off, the display was just a grey canvas surface with no trace of a technological presence. We envision the display to be used for slow-changing information. The device started as a thesis project and has been patented by the institute.

Above right
Interaction-Ivrea and students, end-of-year party interactive facade, June 2004
Because of the peculiar shape of the facade of the student campus (an enormous long and narrow screen), we elected to show videos from the year's work and designed simple interactive displays activated via SMS.

From the outside, the point where interactive design and architecture meet looks very glamorous, with glimpses of fascinating shapes and exciting magic. It is like a cathedral where gifted craftspeople apply their different skills to a common lofty purpose. We imagine a master builder, the guild of stonecutters, painters, glassmakers. From the inside, the cathedral reveals itself to be a set of galleries in a mine. There is no master plan, no master builder; we vaguely follow a lode, digging like moles; there are occasional cave-ins, rare moments of excitement and the occasional nugget. Grisou lurks everywhere, linking mistakes to terrifying consequences.

We thought that we were going to paint frescoes. We found ourselves a thousand feet underground, digging with pick and shovel. Unexpectedly, we find ourselves in the mine – and we like it pretty much.

Notes

1 The institute was founded by Telecom Italia and Olivetti in 2001, and it is now part of the Progetto Italia initiative of Telecom Italia. Through the masters programme and innovation projects developed independently and in partnership with businesses, it acts as a cultural centre disseminating interaction design knowledge and know-how. Further information can be found at www.interaction-ivrea.it

2 We are manic worshippers of George Kubler's *The Shape of Time*. Quoting from it: 'The oldest surviving things made by men are stone tools. A continuous series runs from them to the things of today. The series has branched many times, and it has often run out into dead ends. Whole sequences of course ceased when families or artisans died out or when civilizations collapsed, but the stream of things never was completely stilled. Everything made now is either a replica or a variant of something made a little time ago and so on back without break to the first morning of human time.'

3 To this extent, we are really modern, and our references are Marshall Berman's descriptions of the Crystal Palace, the Brooklyn Bridge, the making of St Petersburg, Rimbaud and Mallarmé in *All that is Solid Melts into Air*. We could define ourselves as Modern because of our ambition, and as Postmodern because of our attitude that cannot escape irony. Thirty years from now, we want to build an airport that embodies Archigram's playful irony, not high-tech arrogance.

4 Who graduated from Interaction-Ivrea in the summer of 2004 with the Acclairism project: for more information see www.acclair.co.uk.

5 And here lies the exceptional value of Interaction-Ivrea, as a place that needs and fosters experiments with their attendant successes and failures. Generally, large established technocentric architectural offices or high-tech corporations couldn't and wouldn't support such an attitude.

6 'Us' stands for a group of predominantly first-year students and professors: Walter Aprile (software), Massimo Banzi (electronic), Stefano Mirti, Chris Noessel (content), Sergio Paolantonio, Jeremy Tai Abbett, and Franziska Huebler (graphic design), with Matteo Pastore and Luca Poncellini (Cliostraat) for space.

7 A finite state automaton (FSA) is a mathematical/computer science construct that has a set of states and some rules that make it change state deterministically based on its previous state and its input. In this case, the FSAS were used to generate arbitrary sequences of blinks in an efficient way. They were also used because they are an elegant formal construct that lends itself naturally to parallelism, and the pulsating lights had to operate in parallel. Any hint of sequentiality would have betrayed the machinery of the space.

8 Stefano Mirti was thesis adviser for both.

9 We know that inflatable spaces have a rich and long history that started with blimps, hit a highly significant moment in 1968 with Archigram's Instant City and the 'Les Structures Gonflables' exhibition in Paris, and produced many interesting buildings, most of them temporary. Many hopes have focused on inflatables, but for practical reasons it seems that we are not living in inflatable houses yet. Still, it is difficult to deny that, if you want to build a prototype environment, the technology that costs less per cubic metre is inflatables. And, if we want to work on a chain of prototype iterations, the inflatables are one of the most interesting solutions. Cheap to buy, easy to make, to change, to fix, to reorganise; they allow mistakes, and maybe even call for them. In this case the group included Walter Aprile and Stefano Mirti plus the energy and passion of Daniele Mancini, Dario Buzzini and Eyal Fried.

10 In this case the group included Walter Aprile and Stefano Mirti plus the energy and passion of Daniele Mancini, Dario Buzzini and Eyal Fried.

11 On this occasion the design team included Walter Aprile, Daniele Mancini and Stefano Mirti. We love doing one-week workshops with external institutions because they force us to explain to others, so we can explain to ourselves. Despite the apparent complexity, mixing design and technology is not difficult. Things you see in glossy magazines can be analysed, learned and improved with surprising ease. Once more, the magic ingredient in the learning is the doing. One week working together has the same effect as 20 lectures or a semester of classes.

12 Radio frequency identification technology consists of tiny cheap tags that can be embedded into objects. These tags contain small amounts of digital information that can be read rapidly, invisibly and without physical contact using radio technology. The simplest form of RFID is systems that prevent store theft; more refined systems can be used to manage inventory, storage and reordering, to build 'smart shelves' in shops, and even as electronic purses. For example, London Transport's Oyster smartcard system is an RFID system. RFID systems can be made much smaller than magnetic systems, can be read from impressive distances and made much more resistant to the physical and electromagnetic environment.

13 The thesis project was developed by Dario Buzzini, tutored by Jan-Christoph Zoels, with Massimo Banzi and Stefano Mirti. During the process of thesis-making, the project produced a commercial prototype for the Prada fashion house. It is currently being developed as an internal project by the institute.

14 We have already mentioned collaboration, and at this stage we can also see it as a specialised form of social competence – an ability that is very difficult to teach, although hints can be given.

15 Professor for new media, arts and design at the University of the Arts in Berlin, designer, co-founder of Art + Com and a brilliant critic.

16 The story starts in Melanesia, during the Second World War. This region of the world was disturbed by the establishment of a series of US bases where cargo planes would arrive loaded with goods. The indigenous people of Vanuatu observed that, before the arrival of the cargo plane, things would happen; the flight controller would climb on the control tower, put on headphones and talk to invisible entities. Afterwards, the plane would arrive. After the US forces left, the inhabitants of Vanuatu tried to make the planes come to the island again, by mimicking the ritual; they lit signal fires on the landing strip, built a bamboo control tower and, wearing half-coconut headphones, muttered into the air. Of course, the Melanesians were perfectly right in their method, as far as they knew. But we know something more: that if we want to build a plane today, we should start by experimenting with gliders, not with a 1:1 painted clay representation of a Boeing 737. On the other hand, we are surrounded by designers who build representations of the future, in the hope that these representations will entice the future into arriving in the shape and colour they want.

17 Everything you see has its internal or external necessity, and if it makes aesthetic or compositional sense, we would never admit we did it on purpose.

18 The exhibition was curated by Massimo Banzi, Edoardo Brambilla, Line Ulrika Christianssen, Holly Coleman, Stefano Mirti and Yaniv Steiner.

19 To tell the whole truth, we are not really interested in polished results. The rough prototype stage is the one that best represents the state of the art in this field. Coming up with apparently perfect solutions is ethically and practically wrong. Roughness is not an option: it is the most appropriate answer to the current problems generated at the meeting point between interaction design and architecture.

20 The design team for Creative Collisions was Anurag Sehgal and Giovanni Cannata, and for Collabolla Jennifer Bove, Simone Pia and Nathan Waterhouse.

21 With Britta Boland and Alberto Jacovoni as thesis adviser.

22 At least with oneself! On the other hand, if you are a freak with no sense of propriety like us, you can also afford to be honest in public … △

Walter Aprile and Stefano Mirti have been teaching, researching and carrying out design work at Interaction-Ivrea for the past three years. Aprile has previously worked in Mexico and the US, and Mirti completed his postdoctoral work in Japan. They are the co-founders of The Italian Job Ltd, a Bangkok-based design studio. For the record, Mirti plays the architect and Aprile acts as the computer geek. More information can be found at www.interaction-ivrea.it

Top

Interaction-Ivrea, 'Interactive Body Snatchers', Salone del Mobile, Milan, 2004

At the Salone del Mobile in Milan, where the international furniture and appliance design world gathers annually, Interaction-Ivrea presented 20 interactive projects by students, faculty and designers who work with the institute. This created a large and mysterious environment, where everything was made to be touched, and where the institute students, staff and faculty were ready to explain and demonstrate. Exhibition design was by the Cliostraat group.

Intelligent Workspaces: Crossing the Thresholds

Lucy Bullivant looks at the shape of the new office to come. With the onset of increasingly sophisticated communications devices, how is the organisation of space in our immediate working environments going to change? Will the lines between furniture and dynamic electronic devices simply blur? Will the structure of commercial office buildings themselves be required to become increasingly reflexive to meet environmental demands in the face of dwindling energy reserves? Or is the mobile nature of electronic communications actually in danger of rendering the permanent office as we know it extinct?

When designing workspaces, architects and designers are all, at some level, driven by the seductive white heat of proliferating technological advances. But this can lead to a lack of socially aware thinking about what is psychologically satisfying in addition to being well resourced and, from the point of view of the boss or employer, performance oriented.

The transition to compactness, lightness, miniaturisation, mobility and greater intelligence in devices for work purposes makes many issues of connectivity important as pervasive computing becomes the norm. The holy grail represented by the potential integration of building, furniture and technology – physical and virtual systems – is a key aspect of this. IBM and Steelcase's BlueSpace interactive and personalised office, and particularly its Everywhere Display, are based on the idea that the distinction between inanimate furniture and dynamic devices will soon blur. But connectivity as an ethically satisfying hybrid of the physical and the virtual is – as very often with such concepts – given less air time.

Certain factors, as widespread as they are superficially attractive, have become compelling smokescreens to the further understanding of this issue. The coming of the PDA (personal digital assistant) has been immensely important to the way work is conducted, enabling, as Chris Luebkeman of Arup, which provides international consultancy in the furtherances of intelligent buildings, describes it, a 'pocket-based workplace in which the workplace goes with you'.[1]

Virtual solutions facilitate the operation and maintenance of devices increasingly used en route on plane or train, or in an airport lounge, coffee bar or at home beyond the still invariably physically defined boundaries of an institutional or corporate spatial context. They offer a beguiling elasticity in behaviour combined with an assertion of the reality that a formally physical workspace is now redundant, as a recent T-Mobile USA advertisement for its wireless HotSpot locations shows. 'Your workforce is mobile. Shouldn't their offices be mobile too?', it reads, showing a hapless man at a computer inside a tiny office, torn from the traditional physical environment we recognise as a workspace and 'beamed down', in *Star Trek* parlance, to the nonplace of an airport departure lounge. In this context, the laughable incongruence of a person working inside a cumbersome shell that would make more space if it were dematerialised underlines the supposed irrelevance of that physical trapping, now that wireless technology offers all the connectivity needed.

We realise, however, that this is not the whole picture, because as users become increasingly WiFi- or Bluetooth-enabled, they also need an appropriate infrastructure within the buildings in which they customarily work – an environmental ecology that offers

Above
T-Mobile USA advertisement for its wireless HotSpot, which allows employees to wirelessly access the office from thousands of designated locations.

However, as the work environment becomes increasingly immanent as well as responsive, it is at the same time far more capable of sensing and monitoring activities. In education, instruction that would once have been physically led is increasingly becoming virtual, and in two to three years' time will come the prospect of examinations being beamed up on the laptop, with results relayed the same way. This smart bubble in the workplace is naturally self-regulating in its own way as well: downloading material from the Web, or sending emails and all other forms of communication, are easily monitored; precise arrival and departure times can be tracked over a long period; and encounters and movement around the building can be observed. So it is not difficult to see the contemporary work environment potentially as a form of invisible panopticon.

There is an irony in the present situation, because just as the advertising rhetoric about smart lifestyle computer products promotes freedom of movement in work habits, advertisements also transcend T-Mobile's joke about the clunky anachronism of a physical office, and show computer users on beaches, mountains or enjoying access in international transit. People are increasingly taking work back with them to do in their home offices as well. But, the fact remains that the protocols governing employees' activities mean that connectivity invariably puts an intelligence net around work modes. The reality of the smart lifestyle offered by enabled environments risks proscribing staff behaviour even more than if we were constantly physically present in offices in between clocking in and clocking out. It has been known for employees to be sacked by email or SMS.

It is possible to see the connectivity imperative as standardising and reductive, in ways that add huge benefit, but which also naturally bring new drawbacks. Facilities managers, if they have a clue, now take full account of new standards to manage the flexibility required by office spaces, bearing in mind diversified work styles. Zigbee, a new global standard enabling a cental wireless building-management system, encompasses wireless switches, monitors, sensors and controls, and gets rid of the need to have extensive cabling to every single light switch, fire alarm or air-conditioning unit.

The risk in a world of pervasive computing is that human instincts become a default position. As Neil Gershenfeld, MIT media director of the Centre of Bits and Atoms, humorously pointed out at 'Flow', the Doors of Perception pervasive computing conference (www.flow.doorsofperception.com) in Amsterdam in 2002: 'You wake up, and your smart house has crashed.' He goes on: 'The next big thing in computers, literally outside the box, is the programmability of the digital world to the rest of the world.'[2] At a 2003 meeting on

a variety of settings with connectivity available when it is required, which demands an integrated environmental design agenda.

In the world of architecture, meanwhile, intelligent-building concepts are slowly grappling with the notion of a building breathing or having a metabolism; and compatible intelligent-building management practices, such as switchable glazing, that save up to 80 per cent of energy loss, are beginning to take root. At best they anticipate the fact that the world is likely to run out of easily accessible oil in eight years' time, with oil prices doubling in eight to 10 years. However, the ecologically adverse effect of the physical baggage of handsets, bulky personal computers, monitors and copiers has been reduced by the arrival of the concept of connectivity, as a desirable and possible way of life in contemporary offices.

making building infrastructure as expressive as Gaudí's physical forms, Gershenfeld explained that 'what jumped out' was the fact 'that building construction is a trillion-dollar-a-year business, and its costs are dominated by labour. They would love to be able to throw away wiring diagrams and have smart lights and thermostats with functions programmed by their users, but that will be doomed if you need a skilled network installer to connect up the lights, and even more doomed if an IT department is needed to keep them lit.' By way of comparison, he points out that 'no one's getting very excited about servers serving services in smart homes, but here's a compelling demand for distributed intelligence'.[3]

It is clear that as the integration of wireless into hi-fi and other consumer devices advances, a metaphorical bridge is being crossed, as interfacing proliferates with so many systems becoming open and distributed via embedded media – ecosystems of devices that 'know' each other intuitively. For the home, firms like Hewlett Packard and Gateway are developing plasma TVs and devices that create a threshold between the PC and media-centre computers due to make the living room the heart of a new digital domestic life. The seamless, wireless home network will be the result of this convergence.

In any focus on making the rather more environmentally complex ecology of workspaces intelligent, it is vital to define what we mean by 'intelligence', especially as it is now fiercely contested by cognitive scientists. It can either denote the brain at the centre, with remote sensing, a legacy of 19th-century thinking, or agent-based action, where every computer has multiple strategies. On its website, Arup says that a building fulfils the definition of being intelligent if 'building fabric, space, services and information systems can respond in an efficient manner to the initial and changing demands of the owner, the occupier and the environment'. Beyond this basic equation defined for client consumption, the perspectives of the user (occupier) on a psychological, anthropological level badly need exploration via creative projects from across the multidisciplinary spectrum in a way that enlarges our sense of what these might be and how they might evolve.

The Design Research Lab (DRL) of the Architectural Association in London, countering the banality of contemporary office design, has developed Corporate Fields, a series of

responsive working environments made over a three-year period, working in collaboration with firms such as Microsoft UK, M&C Saatchi, Razorfish and Arup. The projects, which will be published for the first time in 2005,[4] were evolved by multidisciplinary teams exploiting interconnected design systems. This kind of ethos needs to govern new projects of this kind if they are to be optimally developed.

One factor that parallels the development of the intelligent office is the reality that the amount of personal workspace an employee can count on is getting smaller. In the US, property specialists have confirmed that office space has shrunk in the last decade. While employees – even executives – might have had 300 square feet at their personal disposal 10 years ago, today they are more likely to find themselves in open-plan offices with only between 34 and 36 square feet of working area.[5]

A team of physicists, engineers, scientists and architects at the National Research Council (NRC) in the US has designed a software program that will apparently tell designers whether their office design is pushing the boundaries in terms of being too cramped, too dark, too noisy or too draughty. Its agenda has the banishing of the 'maze' effect of cubicle colonies. To create the software, the NRC researched the most common complaints of people working in open-plan offices. Office planners can now log on to NRC's new online tool, inputting information on partition heights, the amount of workspace, lighting levels and materials proposed. The software then 'calculates physical effects and addresses which features of the design might affect occupant satisfaction most strongly', says the NRC. According to Mark T Greiner, senior vice-president for research, concepts and ventures at Steelcase: 'We were both going after the same holy grail: a way to integrate architecture, furniture and technology, and let users control their environment.'

If the notion of a desk is now increasingly 'hot', that is, on-demand, temporary and, by its very nature, not personal, then many advances are also metamorphosing the longstanding features of the hardware on a desk into a new virtualised or on-demand smart landscape. Softphone, a new type of computer software, allows telephone calls to be made from either Outlook or Notes. Such a development anticipates the eventual future coming of voice-recognition devices, changing the entire procedure of inputting information. In the meantime, the very physical nature of the hand-operated inputting device of the keyboard is challenged by VKB. Industrial designer Paul Priestman's new design for a virtual keyboard uses laser technology to project a full-size keyboard onto any flat surface, and detection software based on optical recognition enabling users

Below
Arup, Work(place) 2010 project, Denver, Colorado, 2003–04
A hotdesk from Arup's Work(place) 2010 project, an office space designed to promote dialogue and showcase issues about the work place.

to tap the images of the keys so that the keyboard behaves like a real one.

A light and soft-edged design not unlike a perfume phial, the keyboard is easily portable, for the concept banishes the notion of a physically weighty and valuable object to lug about and guard along with other luggage. Cabled up, it connects directly to a PDA, mobile phone or computer. VKB's technology can be embedded into other products, so the information is sent via Bluetooth. In other contexts, Priestman (of Priestman Goode) envisages that it could be used for a door entry system, projecting keys onto a wall and switching off when no one is around, or for airport check-in desks, removing the swathe of PCs with their trailing cables. Because its presence is 'on demand' and determined by a switch, the desk becomes free of one major piece of hardware that has been part of the family of desktop objects for some years, a process that moved on to a further stage when computers became the currently predominant LCDs in vertical form. Priestman sees future applications for VKB in putting the screen into the back of an airline or train seat, or designing café tables with the screen built into them, as screens are becoming much more personalised.

The VKB high-performance interface will soon be embedded in a wide array of communications, computing and entertainment devices, including mobile phones, PDAs, ultralight notebook

computers, gaming consoles, interactive TV set-top boxes, digital media gateways and many touchscreen applications, says its manufacturer, i.Tech Dynamic (part of Hutchison Harbour Ring Ltd, in turn part of Hutchison Whampoa, the 30th largest company in the world, with four manufacturing facilities in China).

It is good that counter-design proposals have been made by designers like Dunne & Raby and Kitchen Rogers Design (KRD) that question the normative assumptions underlying the way technology is utilised in the work place. KRD's RAT (Rogue Ambience Table) prototype, designed in 2001 in collaboration with Dominic Robson, and sponsored by IDEM (a furniture company previously part of the Hille group), exploits the theme of how we use technology as a screen to manage our lifestyles and public image. The system, exhibited at both '100% Design' and 'Workplace', two trade fairs staged in 2001, includes a telephone and a selection of sound cubes. By positioning a particular cube to emit the background sound of their choice (driving in a fast car, club music, birds chirruping), users can give callers the impression that they are somewhere more exotic than the office. The cheeky acronym RAT signifies the power to deceive and be undercover in other places. With the coming of video mobile phones that will hamper this form of fiction, KRD's design, which has so far received enquiries from a number of galleries, offers a polemical palliative to the potentially chilly transparency of pervasive computing.

Whether or not the parameters of such a project transcend the limitations of the impersonal 'cubicle farms' of the modern office chronicled in Scott Adams'

Above
Paul Priestman/Priestman Goode, VKB **virtual keyboard, 2004**
Laser technology allows the totem-like VKB to project a computer keyboard onto a flat surface, desk or café table.

comic strip *Dilbert* remains to be seen. In an attempt to address the myriad of issues connected with partition-based offices and re-empower employees in the face of this growing breed of environment, Adams approached the international user-centred design consultancy IDEO (www.ideo.com) with a proposal for Dilbert's Ultimate Cubicle. For weeks designers in the firm's San Francisco office lived in a dizzyingly Dilbertesque maze of identical offices as preparation for a series of prototypes. The result was a modular cubicle allowing each worker to select the components from a kit of parts, and create a space based on his or her personal tastes and lifestyle.

The modules include a seat, computer and a display (complete with 'boss monitor'). Potential floor modules include artificial grass, shag carpet and tatami mats, and light modules mimic the sun's movement patterns of glowing and fading with the rhythm of the day. Punching bags, a hammock that nestles away until needed, and an aquarium are all items available from the catalogue, which has been designed so that the occupant can find the combination of modules that best fits their working style.

Interior projects like Grand Hotel Salome by Ron Arad (see pages 54–61) or Tobi Schneidler's ReFashion Lab (pages 72–8) explore the impact of the fusion of new technologies with different types of space: in the case of Salome, the leisure space of a hotel, a place in which millions of people are used to working on location, and with FashionLab, the function of the space is to sell clothes and promote fashion. While these typically more leisure-oriented environments become more intelligent, the spatial identity of the workspace and public building interior is not simply becoming a shell in which converging technologies must be on hand. Designers are

transforming it into an integrated system of structure and media.

SmartSlab™, for instance, is a multimedia display system that is also an extremely tough, 60-square-centimetre, 7.5-centimetres deep modular structural tile. It was developed by the principal of b consultants, Tom Barker, a design engineer responsible for many multidisciplinary projects in the fields of industrial design, engineering, technology and architecture over the last 14 years, who became professor and head of the Department of Industrial Design Engineering at the Royal College of Art in 2004. SmartSlab's™ pixels are arranged in a honeycomb pattern. The units can be combined to create small installations or huge display walls. The product attracted the early interest of London Underground, which may use it for dynamic

Above
Kitchen Rogers Design (KRD) with Dominic Robson, RAT (Rogue Ambience Table), 2001
Ab Rogers using the RAT, a range of sound cubes and a telephone, to set up sound 'camouflage' for users. He can choose from driving in a fast car, club music, birds chirruping, and other options, to give the impression he is on location.

Right and opposite
IDEO and Scott Adams, Dilbert's Ultimate Cubicle, 2003–04
Designed for Scott Adams (pictured), the comic-strip artist responsible for *Dilbert*, together with IDEO, San Francisco, the cubicle reinvents the typical partition-based office as a more welcoming and empowering space that employees can personalise.

signage, and the Richard Rogers Partnership is considering it for Heathrow's Terminal 5 and the firm's Barcelona Bullring project. Zaha Hadid's Tokyo Guggenheim, a competition her architectural practice won in 2002, will feature a 600-square-metre SmartSlab™ display for art and information built into the surface of the building. Inspired by the naturally efficient optics of a fly's eye, the display's hexagonal pixels enable a finer image quality than one that is a standard square, with the light-emitting diode within capable of covering 16 million possible colours. Moving and still images on the display are controlled by a standard PC system using custom SmartSlab™ software.

Barker explains that the design 'can be customised to provide digital systems, including sensors detecting people standing on the panels and changing the displayed images in response'. Direct Internet-feeds with customised content for tagged or subscribed viewers is another option, as well as a 'finger painting' mode to allow people to 'draw' or 'graffiti' on the panels. Lastly, it is envisaged that viewer dwell-time recording 'for commercial purposes' through proximity detectors is also an option, giving the product a potential surveillance aspect. While SmartSlab™ is not specifically intended for office spaces, it is clearly suitable for educational and community buildings, public places and foyers, anywhere with a need for ambient visuals that could quite naturally involve different types of work or task-related activities. It is an example of a new initiative for the urban digital environment, demonstrating one way in which the omniscience of pervasive computing may take form in the future.

Its integration is clearly a polemical issue, as computing has now become social infrastructure, as Malcolm McCullough, author of *Digital Ground:*

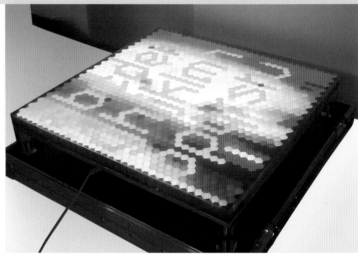

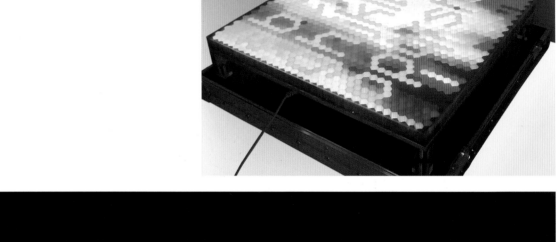

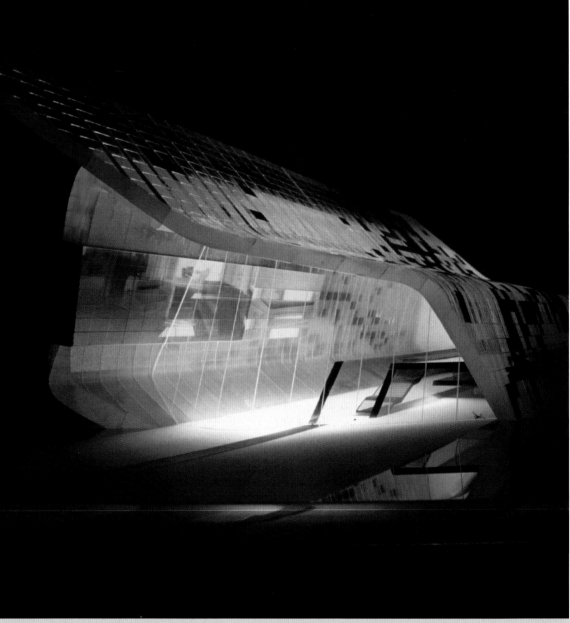

Top

Tom Barker/b consultants, SmartSlab™, 2001
A single slab of the SmartSlab™ multimedia display system, seen here in text mode. The slabs can be combined to create small installations or huge display walls with moving and still images controlled by software. The design can be customised to detect people standing on the panels, a finger-painting mode allows people to draw or graffiti on the panels, and there is the option for direct Internet-feeds to provide customised content for tagged or subscribed viewers.

Bottom

Zaha Hadid Architects, winning design for the new Tokyo Guggenheim art gallery, 2002
The project includes a 600-square-metre SmartSlab™ display for art and information built into the surface of the building.

Opposite

Robert Cohen/Archiram, Pixel City, 2003
Robert Cohen's Pixel City visualisation of a SmartSlab™ building fusing architecture, advertising and corporate image, was produced as part of the group's Virtual Architecture project.

Architecture, Pervasive Computing and *Environmental Knowing,*[6] has said. Being pervasive, or ubiquitous, SmartSlab™ cannot be switched off, and the challenge is in some ways cognitive flow management. As IDEO's Colin Burns says (in the firm's recent publication *Smart Spaces*): 'Technology should be interwoven.' This is already a very strategic procedure. The design of Heathrow's Terminal 5 buildings (due for completion in 2008), for which Arup is in charge of the core infrastructure for the communications, IT systems and networks, applies the new potential of wireless LAN (local area network), firstly at an operational level, and secondly through customer service and experience. The plan is to put in a single infrastructure that will make more functions intelligent, for example introducing a mobile check-in with a hand scanner.

There are huge advantages to the generation of a greater degree of interoperability, for example with roads and canals (which are communication systems), setting up standard networks, and having operating systems that can self-repair (at IBM 95 per cent of the research budget apparently goes into autonomous computing). However, the problematic onward march of civilian surveillance systems is always an issue, along with the notion of standard networks. Anyone wanting to think

about one aspect of this more thoroughly, might well look at the growth of RFIDs (radio frequency ID tags), minute computer circuitry now invading retailing (and items of clothing; they are used in Prada's Manhattan store designed by OMA), which reveal many levels of consumer behaviour to manufacturers and raise privacy scenarios of an even wider nature.[7]

Going beyond issues of productivity, The Disappearing Computer project,[8] a European Union-funded initiative, specifically looks at how collections of artefacts can act together to produce new behaviour and functionality, and to ensure that people's experience in these new environments can be coherent and engaging. This is critical, as the borders between the physical and nonphysical fade and, as human beings, we try to match ourselves to the 'second nature' of our technological contexts. The intelligence incorporated into the work place must be holistically framed, and about people as well as profit through productivity, using communication enhancement and other euphemistically defined factors merely as tools. Workspaces are often revamped regularly, but without a strong relationship between hard and soft design issues. To facilitate credible, creative projects that transform the contemporary work place, architects and designers need to continue advancing the art of multidisciplinary team working, contextualising proposals and questioning the brief to allow new potentials to emerge. △

Notes
1 Conversation with Chris Luebkeman, Alan Newbold, Duncan Wilson and Jim Read at Arup, 27 May 2004. With thanks to them and to Tony Dunne of Dunne & Raby (conversation on 31 August 2004) for informal discussions about some of these issues.
2 See 'Personal Fabrication: A Talk with Neil Gershenfeld', The Edge Foundation, www.edge.org, 24 July 2003.
3 Ibid.
4 Brett Steele, *Corporate Fields: Office Projects by the* AA *Design Research Lab,* AA Publications (London), 2005.
5 Source: GWL Realty Advisors, Vancouver.
6 MIT Press, 2004.
7 Josh McHugh, 'Attention Shoppers', *Wire,* July 2004, p150.
8 www.disappearing-computer.net

TERRAIN VAGUE

Interactive Space and the Houscape

'Only connect!' Despite the proliferation of interactivity technologies for domestic spaces, current commercial models for the smart house remain focused on the supply of gizmos and multimedia flatscreens. What is the design potential for connectivity in the home? Mike Weinstock asks how interactive technologies might achieve a new level of topographical and environmental change and enhance the spaces in which we live.

The coupling of space, technology and domesticity is part of our architectural legacy, an unregarded inheritance that extends beyond the *machine à habiter* of Le Corbusier. It includes the spatial differentiation of the *Raumplan* of Loos, the continuous connectivity of space of Mies, the transformable space of Rietveld's Schröder House, and the source of Modernist theory, the traditional Japanese House. These concepts are persistent, but rarely considered to be relevant today, and the slow reduction of the phenomenal complexity of the Modernist spatial agenda in favour of a simplified goal of efficiency of means and functions has brought us to a condition in which the union of interactivity and the idea of a home are seen as unlikely collaborators.

Space and time are inextricably entwined in the idea of a home. The anthropologist Mary Douglas argued in 'The Idea of a Home' that a home cannot be defined by its functions, but is a 'pattern of regular doings', and 'neither the space nor its appurtenances have to be fixed, but there is something regular about the appearance and reappearance of its furnishings'.[1] People come and go, flowing through a home; however, there are some regularities or patterns that give it a structure in time. A home is an organisation of space that has some structure in time, in which people interact in a pattern of events and phenomena that integrate space and perceptions.

In the domestic realm, interactivity now tends to mean a multitude of media connections and applications, resulting in spaces that are mediated yet somehow remote from our senses, in which phenomenal qualities are muted and in which time is 'real' yet never realised as experience. The 'real time' of media connectivity is a paradox, muting our phenomenal presence in the physical world but extending our connection to the constantly unfolding data image of the world, in which each second has the capacity to carry an infinitely extended array of data and images. In real time we are alone, though always reachable and accountable. Ways of working and living have grown up around mediated interactivity so that personal physical space is increasingly unmarked by the daily and seasonal changes of light and temperature in the physical world. Real time is unlocated, and tends to induce a corresponding perceptual dislocation from the physical space in which we are present.

The space in which we live has become a *terrain vague*, and our fascination with its dislocation is a measure of its availability for the contemporary imagination, part of the exploratory engagement, both topographical and theoretical, with spaces 'in between', with vectors of ambiguity and with fluid boundary conditions. At its most extreme, the space of the home is a space of transit, between the digital and physical worlds, between the infinite extension of data connectivity and the compression of phenomenally mute and depersonalised physical space.

Marc Auge's anthropological analysis, set out in *Non Places*,[2] deals with urban spaces and programmes, but it can be extended to current modes of interactivity and to current built domestic space. The materiality of the boundaries between interior and exterior, between public and private, is no longer solid and opaque. Excess individualisation has destabilised the reference points of collective identity, a paradoxical counterpoint to the acceleration of global culture. Supermodernity produces 'urban' spaces that are not places. Non-places have programmes that typically have a structured time of occupation, and are related to networks of information or movement. They are transit zones to which the individual purchases rights for measured units of time. In Auge's argument, places are related to dwelling, social interchange and spoken language; nonplaces are related to transit, assemblies of solitude, and communication by codes and images. Auge understood nonplaces to be airports and stations,

bedroom   studio 01   circulation   bathroom   toilet   ramp   garage   storage   meeting room   circulation   kitchen   verandah   living room   fire place

N

Opposite
UN Studio, Möbius House, Het Gooi, the Netherlands, 1993–8
The house is orientated east to west, and the phenomenal character of the surrounding forest and garden infiltrates it through a long glass wall on the south side, providing a mode of interaction with the environment that is integrated with programmatic deployment of spatial characteristics. As the Möbius loop turns inside out the materialisation follows, glazed details and concrete structural elements swap roles as glazed facades are put in front of the concrete construction, dividing walls are made of glass, and furniture such as tables and stairs is made of concrete.

Above right
The plan reveals the spatial loop that enables the house to form its relationship to the landscape. By being stretched to the maximum, rather than displaying a compact or tall shape, the house organises the spatial quality of the interior in relation to the external environment. The mathematical model of the Möbius is not literally transferred to the building, but can be found in architectural ingredients, such as the light, the staircases and the way in which people move through the house.

Right
Space and time are inextricably entwined in the idea of a home.
The diagram organises the intertwining paths of two people running their own trajectories but sharing certain moments, and maps the 24-hour cycle of sleeping, working and living. As a representation of 24 hours of family life, the double-locked torus acquires a time-space dimension, and integrates programme, circulation and structure seamlessly.

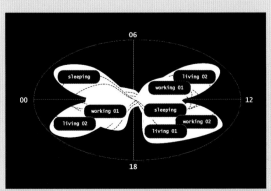

but the description is now alarmingly close to many contemporary forms of housing.

The separation of the architectural discourses of technology, personal space and domesticity from the everyday experience of life is an equally persistent theme in other cultural areas. The global 'information society', and the anxieties that surround it, have been prefigured in films and literature throughout the last century. EM Forster presented a disquiet about the implications for personal relationships and the loss of personal contact resulting from remote communication technology. In a short story, *The Machine Stops* (1909), a worldwide machine supplies all the essentials of life. People live alone in underground cells; they seldom meet anyone face to face, but communicate by means of a globally networked system of 'optic plates' and telephones. The protagonist of the story becomes obsessed with the phrase 'Only connect!'. He escapes to the unoccupied surface, and comes to realise that there is a difference between mediated experience and direct perception:

'I see something like you in this plate but I do not see you. I hear something like you through this telephone, but I do not hear you.'[3]

A humorous commentary is presented in the films of Jaques Tati, in which Monsieur Hulot's bemused confrontations with a technology that he fails to interact with strikes a particular resonance with us. In *Mon Oncle*, Hulot is lonely and unemployed, and goes to live with his sister and her husband in a fully automated home that is impersonal, uncomfortable, unreliable and, ultimately, alienating. The theme here is not so much dystopian, but more how technology makes us do ridiculous things. Dystopian anxieties are strongly marked in literature and films, as if a measure of the anticipated effectiveness of any new technology is the peculiar mixture of dread and excitement it engenders; there is a narcotic dimension to society's dreams of interacting with technology.

Two interesting built experiments reveal different aspects of interactivity, and both utilise continuous computational comparisons between digital models and events in the physical world. Although quite different in their aims, and indeed in their

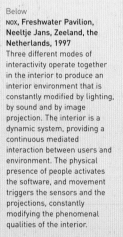

Below
NOX, Freshwater Pavilion, Neeltje Jans, Zeeland, the Netherlands, 1997
Three different modes of interactivity operate together in the interior to produce an interior environment that is constantly modified by lighting, by sound and by image projection. The interior is a dynamic system, providing a continuous mediated interaction between users and environment. The physical presence of people activates the software, and movement triggers the sensors and the projections, constantly modifying the phenomenal qualities of the interior.

computational processes, in combination they demonstrate a potential means of achieving a more spatial and temporal interactivity. The Aegis Hypo-Surface of dECOi is a programmable wall or surface, which can be deformed by pneumatic pistons and springs. The ability to reconfigure the surface of the wall is achieved by a complex mechanical system of linked pistons and springs that move the metal strips of the wall. The wall requires a static structural frame behind the movable surface, to carry all of the dynamic structural load, and the springs attached to it ensure that the activated pistons are returned to their neutral condition. A central computer analyses the acoustical changes in the environment, and responds to these stimuli by sending signals to each individual piston to produce complex patterns on the surface. The wall interacts spatially with the environment.

Three different modes of interactivity operate together in the interior of the Freshwater Pavilion by NOX. Together these produce an interior environment that is constantly modified by lighting, sound, and by image projection. The space does not change topographically or in dimension, but in a limited sense it is programmable. In this case, rather than responding to sound by a single computer driving hundreds of activators, the Freshwater systems respond to the movement of people within the space. An array of sensors and trackers is coupled to multiple distributed processors, which produce interference in the continuous processing of a virtual real-time model of water. Sensed changes in the environment produce changes in the virtual water system, images from which are projected into the interior space of the pavilion.

There are interesting innovations here, not least in the distributed intelligence of multiple processors, but what is significant is not the qualities of the interior environment, nor even the real-time immediacy and content of the images projected, but the conceptual schema of interactivity. Firstly, the continuous process of calculating the parameters and performance of the digital model of an active body of water is modified by information from the physical world and, secondly, the physical environment is directly modified by those changes to the digital model.

The means of achieving topographical and environmental change to architectural space exist, albeit in experimental form. The question that must be asked is to what agenda can these technologies be coupled to enhance the quality

of the spaces in which we live? If we are to replace the *terrain vague* of the contemporary home with a more explicit cartography, we must start with an examination of the models of home that are part of our architectural legacy.

The traditional Japanese house provided a model for Modernist architects and theoreticians. In particular they valued the way in which the material construction suggested a continuity of interior and exterior. It was not just a single unit subdivided according to programme, and although some Modernist accounts refer mainly to the plan, the section was the principal ordering device. The section was spatially and materially differentiated, by a 'high' area for dwelling and sleeping and a 'lower' part – the working space and kitchen. The floor of the higher part was covered with boards or tatami; the lower part formerly had a floor of stamped earth and is still often known as a *niwa* (garden or courtyard). Space was structured around social practices, and was related to traditional ideas of land use and demarcation in agriculture. It was an arrangement of separate but related spaces that together constructed a 'housescape'.

The relationship of the spatial organisation to material construction was manifested by the flexibility of division in the principal interior space, and by the continuity of material construction between interior and exterior. The horizontal was emphasised by the way in which material is carried through from one space to another, from interior to exterior. The main spatial divisions were part of this arrangement, but there were also movable partitions of paper on wooden frames (*shoji*), which slid along grooved sills and lintels. Interior floors were often extended through to the exterior to form a veranda, which was considered to be both interior and exterior space.

Above right
Angelo Invernizzi, Casa Girasole, Verona, Italy, 1935
Each wheel is a metre high, and sits between the upper part of the house and the roof level of the lower part. The house has two levels, one fixed and the other rotating to follow the arc of the sun, maximising the light in the interior. The top level contains the main living space.

Two other models provide the instruments for a more detailed mapping of the operating concepts of the 'housescape': the Müller Villa by Loos, and the Schröder House by Rietveld. The Müller Villa is a simple cube with a complex interior set of spaces, each of which has differing dimensions according to what Loos considered to be the hierarchy of programmatic importance. The *Raumplan* was a spatial structure that used sectional differentiation as the main ordering device, so that storeys merge into one another to produce continuous space. The largest is the main living space, which Loos called the 'residential hall', and its two-storey volume is linked to all the other spaces – the dining room, boudoir and study, and at the higher level to bedrooms and terraces.

Programme subdivisions such as 'boudoir' may have limited relevance today, but topographical differentiation coupled with continuity is still important. The upper floor of the Schröder House has a system of sliding partitions that allow the reconfiguration of the space according to need, and although there are severe limitations to the character and functionality of the variety of available spaces produced by manual reconfiguration, there is a capacity to produce daily or even more frequent spatial changes.

The pattern of living is a little different today, and the integration of work and domesticity occurs in varying degrees, across all professions. Families split and recombine, people come and go, and the desire for private space within families is matched by the increasing number of single people living in shared homes. An extra bedroom, or space for a work project, may be necessary for a few days or weeks, whilst other domestic shared spaces may need to be more permanent. Internet, telecommunications and media activity may be private or shared, or cycle between these modes. Far from negating the need for structures in time, the new housescape needs the pattern of phenomena of light and dark, of daily and seasonal changes, to maintain its identity and its continuity.

The Möbius House, built by UN Studio, uses an interesting new mode of topographical differentiation, and recognises one of the new patterns of living and working that have emerged. The organising principle is a mathematical model that has one single continuous surface: the Möbius strip. The twisting figure of eight is used to provide space in which two people can work apart, yet meet together at certain times in what become shared spaces. The husband and wife, both of whom work at home, have separate work areas, and the shared domestic spaces of family and social life are enfolded by the continuous surface structure. The house is orientated east to west, and the phenomenal character of the surrounding forest and garden infiltrates it through a long glass wall on the south side. Interaction with the environment is passive in Möbius, although well integrated with programmatic deployment of special characteristics.

In the Casa Girasole built by Angelo Invernizzi in Verona, Italy, in 1935, there is a more positive interactivity with the environment. The house has two levels, one fixed and the other rotating to follow the arc of the sun, maximising the light in the interior. 'Il Girasole' has a simple programme, built as a holiday home, but the rotating top level contains the main living space. The plan is interesting, not occupying the full circle that a rotating device suggests, but rather a chevron-like arrangement of two rectangular wings, leaving three-quarters of the circle as a garden over which the two-storey top rotates.

The union of these ideas sets out the spatial and phenomenal parameters for the contemporary housescape. Spatial organisation needs to be flexible to adapt to changing patterns of life and work. The coupling of interactive surface technology to topographical differentiation would provide a means of activating subtle changes to the physical dimensions and varying degrees of separation and privacy that are demanded by fluctuating programmatic needs. The cycling between public or private media interactivity lies between spatial and environmental patterns, needing to be linked to both. The interactivity of the internal phenomenal character to the external environment can be orchestrated in complex patterns that are active, and may enable a new agenda of environmental adaptability aligned to another spatial flexibility, providing spaces that get taller, lighter and more open in the summer, cosier and warmer, or smaller in the winter. Housescapes will require distributed intelligence and active material systems, programmable virtual representations of themselves (digital models) that are capable of changing their internal parameters and performances in relation to the life of their inhabitants and events in the external world. ∆

Notes
1 Mary Douglas, 'The Idea of a Home: A Kind of Space', *Social Research*, Vol 58, spring 1991.
2 Marc Auge, *Non-Places: An Introduction to an Anthropology of Supermodernity*, Verso (New York), 1995.
3 EM Forster, 'The Machine Stops' (1909), in *The Eternal Moment and Other Stories*, first published by Harcourt, Brace & World, Inc, 1928, Universal Library Edition, Grosset & Dunlap (New York), 1956.

Michael Weinstock is an architect. He was born in Germany, and lived as a child in the Far East and then West Africa, where he attended an English public school. At the age of 17 he ran away to sea after reading Conrad. During his years at sea in traditional sailing ships he gained experience in shipyards and shipbuilding. He studied architecture at the Architectural Association and has taught at the AA School of Architecture since 1989. He is co-founder and co-director, with Michael Hensel, of the Emergent Technologies and Design masters programme, and co-founder of the research practice Emergence and Design Group. He has organised symposia, curated exhibitions, lectured and published widely on architectural, urban and technical issues.

Media House Project: the House is the Computer, the Structure is the Network

A multidisciplinary team of more than a hundred people developed the Media House, a prototype of a domestic living space unveiled in Barcelona in 2001, writes **Lucy Bullivant**. The project is a technologically advanced interface for interaction that is a benchmark of its kind.

Spanish architect Vicente Guallart, director of the IaaC (Institut d'arquitectura avançada de Catalunya) and the Metapolis architectural studio, argues that the new technologies of information and communication have already transformed the home into a microcity, a genuinely multifunctional environment from which the global village can be reached. Soon, he says, 'the passive physical world defined by purely functional structures which give people shelter, and in which we consume products and interact with the world by way of screens, will be rendered obsolete by intelligent environments'. A key feature of these will be the fact that 'everyone and everything – people, objects and spaces – will both generate and consume information, and ideally, transform it into knowledge'.

The Media House[1] is an attempt to build a prototype of a domestic living space in which both physical and digital space exist simultaneously, 'in a process of constant feedback in which both worlds learn from each other's and their own potentialities and limitations'.

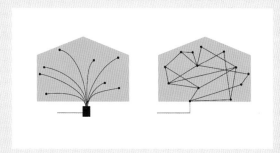

Top
A house with a computer (left), and the house as the computer (right).

Bottom left and right
The structure of the Media House needed to be a system integrating structure and infrastructure, as well as the information network. The team devised SIDWIS, a hybrid system meaning Structure Infrastructure Data-Way Integrated System, in the form of a very slender geodesic form, easy to assemble, dismount and transport. A profile of a EUTRAC data bus track, a wooden and aluminium structure incorporating data and electrical networks, is doubly hybrid, including two lines for the low-speed transmission of information.

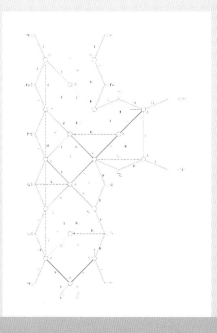

It aims to be a platform facilitating culture, education and common sense, as team member Enric Ruiz Geli describes it. Architecture, he feels, as an organiser of human activity through the construction of space, 'has the potential to play a key role in this new, hybrid situation by redefining itself as an interface for interaction'.

The team included the Metapolis architectural studio, the IaaC, Elisava design school, the I2CAT consortium and the Media Lab at MIT – architects, computer programmers, audiovisual-makers, physicist Neil Gershenfeld (at the time director of the Things that Think consortium at MIT's Media Lab), and the UPC anthropologist Artur Serra – and later expanded to over a hundred people[2] inputting ideas, technologies and resources.

The intention was to test information technologies beyond the sphere of the computer and integrate them into everyday life, without creating a space cluttered by technology. According to Josep Ferrer I Llop, rector of the Universitat Politècnica de Catalunya: 'This involved thinking about how the media could be integrated into the physical space, what services could be supplied to the domestic space via the Internet, and the relationship between physical and information structure.' The team wanted to build computers from the components of buildings, so that 'the logical intelligence of a structure can grow with its physical form'. By means of a single microprocessor, multiple tiny computer chips were inserted inside different objects and elements of the house.

The information structure, thanks to distributed computing, incorporated the physical structure, electrical and data networks. The house's objects, elements, space, people and networks are, via information protocols – such as nerve cells in the human body – able to communicate with each other in what Eric Ruiz Geli calls a

'common language', using the actual structure of the building as a data support'. As a result, the house became the computer, the structure the network. 'All the architecture finds itself in a kind of electrical synergy,' Geli adds. 'It's not the software industry that creates, from the outside, a juxtaposed system to the house but, on the contrary, it is the house, the inhabitants and the objects – the ones who work, dialogue, relate to randomness, chaos, to control and to all the complexity that we may wish.'

The project included an analysis of the properties of the different environmental layers of the house: users, space, objects, networks, limits and contents (for example, light, music, video, painting). This meant there was scope to make the information in the structure as expressive as its physical form. Field research analysed the relationship between inhabitants, dwelling units and time, considering degrees of complexity in the ways in which spaces responded to occupation. This then gave the project the scope to 'define the concept of movement as a key factor in the

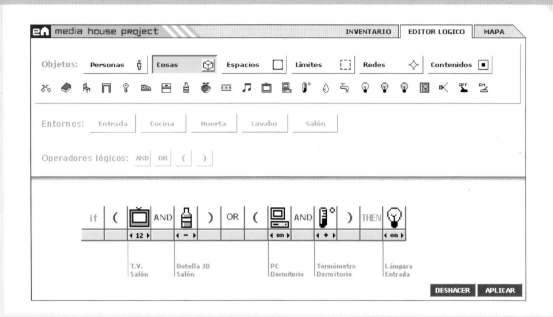

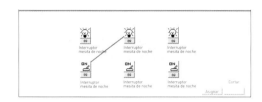

Top and bottom right
The Home Web provides the
status of all the elements in a
home, shown as a digital world
equivalent with data or as a
virtual representation of
physical space, and is able to
link them using logical
phrases. In the digital world,
the hierarchies of the physical
world do not exist – the
structure is flattened out, so
the properties of objects can
be linked, directly affecting the
property of the whole home or
city. 'In the future we should
be able to qualify the
relationships that we create
between things.'

Notes
1 *Media House Project: the
House is the Computer, the
Structure is the Network*, was
published as a book by the
IaaC, Barcelona, in 2004.
2 Media House directors:
Vicente Guallart, Enric Ruiz-
Geli, Willy Müller. Structure:
Max Sanjulian. Coordinator:
Ariadna Cantis. Collaborators:
Neil Gershenfeld (director,
Center for Bits and Atoms, MIT
Media Lab), Pau Roig
(Fundació Politècnica de
Catalunya), Artur Serra
(I2CAT), Nuria Díaz (director of
the interfaces masters course,
Elisava), Manuel Gausa
(president of Metapolis), Mercè
Sala (president, Fundació
Politècnica de Catalunya).
gRAm: Susana Noguero.
Nodes and integration: Michel
Oltramare. Housing X-ray:
Laura Cantarella. As the team
in total numbered over a
hundred, for a full list of
credits see *Media House
Project*, op cit.
3 For background information on
Internet 0, see http://cba.mit.
edu/projects/I0/I0.pdf

generation of new spatiality', as team members
Silvia Banchini, Maurizio Bonizzi and Giovanni
Franceschelli (responsible for structural
typologies) put it.

The space of the house, once understood as
relations in metric or anthropological
dimensions, becomes 'identifiable in social,
psychological and sensorial dimensions', and
needs 'ever more reactive fields or surfaces that
provoke tactile, olfactory, visible and auditory
sensations'. One spatial structure can house a
LAN (local area network) that can read and
recombine all the bits of information present
both inside and outside the space.

The Media House, presented for the first time
to the public in a 'Digital Day' staged at the
Mercat de les Flors, Barcelona, on 27 September
2001, broached many lines of research of high
prospective value to the way people may think
about, construct and inhabit dwellings in the
future. These include the value of distributed
computation systems; the model of a future
house being more akin to a tree than a building
in the way its various structures relate to each
other and to the context; and using materials in
the house that incorporate intelligent systems in
their actual mass, and thereby cease to be inert
– rendering the house a place that can
potentially continue to manufacture itself. It also
encompasses the issue of the space of the house
as a potential open system of plug-and-play
activities, networked neighbourhoods, the
physicality of a mediatised space, space-to-
space video conferencing, and sensorial

interfaces making the dwelling aware, learning to
react to the requests of the environment.

After the launch, the Media Lab at MIT created a
research group called Internet 0,[3] directed by
Gershenfeld, and members of the team made further
smaller-scale projects dealing with the theme of the
informational house. Sociópolis, a new residential
community being developed by Guallart in Valencia,
will share some of the Media Lab's resources, including
a website for the residents. Media House was clearly
one of the most major initiatives of its kind. It would be
well worth looking at its approach in a few years' time
to evaluate what aspects prove the most desirable,
and which could be replaced for reasons of changing
needs or technological advances. ∆

The IaaC, an institute born out of an active collaboration between the
government of Catalonia and the civic association Metapolis, has a core
interest in interacting with institutions, organisations and companies on the
local, national and international levels. It operates as a polyvalent centre of
international reference, oriented towards research development, education
and the diffusion of an advanced architecture. Theoretical approaches range
from an interactive vision of architecture and technology to dynamic large-
scale proposals. The impact of new information technologies on living space
is explored in the media architecture course. Real-scale prototypes are
constructed in order to experiment with the integration of communication
technologies into the physical spaces of the domestic environment by means
of new interfaces using advanced data networks, integrating information into
everyday life and approaching the construction of new spatial and information
structures through the optimum combination of intelligent logic and physical
form. www.metapolis.com

'There Has Always Been a Relationship Between Design and Technology'

Ron Arad on Interactivity and Low-Res Design

Above right
Lolita chandelier, Gio' Marconi Gallery, Milan, 2004, and 'Nine Positions', the British pavilion, 9th Venice Architecture Biennale, 2004
The chandelier Arad designed for Swarovski is made of a crystal pixel board, spiral in shape, and omnidirectional. It links to viewers' mobile phones via SMS. It includes 2,100 crystals, 1,050 white LEDS, a kilometre of nine-way cable braid shielding and 31 processors.

Best known for his tactile and colourful furniture designs, Ron Arad also experiments with multimedia technologies in his interactive installations and built work. **Lucy Bullivant** talks to Arad and discovers how he transfers the pleasures of one medium over to another: his impulse to 'bounce' physical objects such as his tempered steel 'rolling shells', translating into low-res interactive responses on demand – a technological tactility.

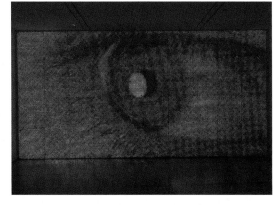

Sensuous man-made materials can now be harnessed to new technologies, and transformed into unique interfaces for communication. In Lo-rez-dolores-tabula-rasa,[1] an installation designed by architect and designer Ron Arad and exhibited during the Milan Furniture Fair in 2004, was a unique form of screen (a giant 8 x 4 metre wall) made out of pieces of Corian® (a man-made solid surface material) embedded with 37,127 fibre-optic pixels. This became a filter for film and still images projected onto its surface. Because of the screen's translucency, the images appeared in low-res, with fine lines Arad likens to 'topographical lines on a map'. In a process of 'planting the moving picture in the material, the film is being sent to the depths of the Corian®'. The entire room turned into an immersive film it was hard to leave. Kurt Forster, the curator of the 9th Venice Architecture Biennale, certainly agreed, including it in the atmospheric Episodes display sequence there in the autumn of 2004.

Such is the pulling power of the alchemical designs Arad creates: his interest in design straddles three and four dimensions seemingly effortlessly. By filtering technology in this way, he forces it to become something tactile and experiential, in the process creating an entirely new concept for transmitting film. 'When you look at any LCD screen, if it's not switched on, it's like a black hole – very dense. But here we can have a tactile, perfect white wall which is beautiful in itself, smooth and stucco-like. You can always tell when something's a projection or a plasma screen. But I don't think there's ever been a real surface like this, which has the ability to transmit film and images.'

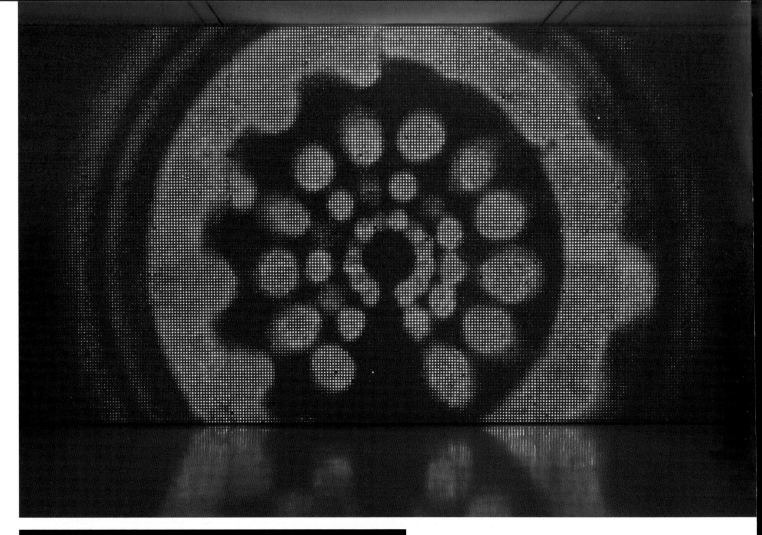

depth of the wall, and you think you see running
messages – or are there people inside?'

It's hardly surprising that many of Arad's installations
are event based, given that he was a student of Bernard
Tschumi's at the Architectural Association. They are also
always very simple. Lolita,[2] a chandelier for Swarovski,
first shown at the Gio' Marconi Gallery in Milan in 2004,
is made of a crystal pixel board, spiral in shape, and
therefore omnidirectional. This took him immediately to
the next decision: to link it to everyone's mobile phone via
SMS. But it is no ordinary chandelier; it possesses 2,100
crystals, 1,050 white LEDs, a kilometre of nine-way cable
braid shielding, and 31 processors. Peter Cook included
the piece in 'Nine Positions', the British Pavilion exhibition
on UK architecture at the 9th Venice Biennale,
scrawling on the gallery wall the appropriate mobile
number visitors needed to ring to set off a reaction in the
chandelier. He aptly describes Arad as 'inevitably drawn

Corian® is often used in an everyday fashion
– for example, for kitchen table tops – but Arad
also designed a table in the material shaped like
a lens, with 22,000 fibre-optic pixels embedded
in its form, which serves as another 'recipient'
of a choice of media images.

This fusion of material and media was an
exciting experience to witness, as Arad predicted.
When people entered the Gallery Gio' Marconi
in Milan, they encountered the imposing tactile,
satin-smooth structures embedded with fibre
optics. 'Then, just when you are not looking,'
says Arad, 'moving messages emerge from the

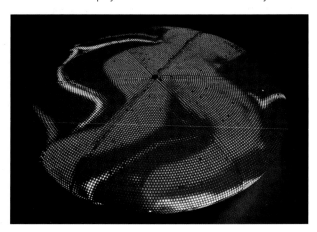

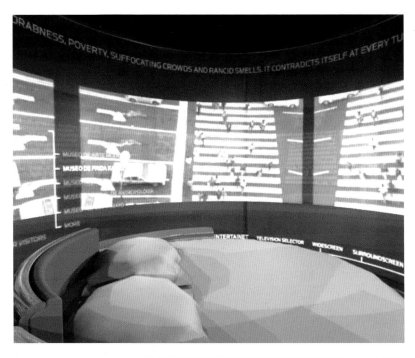

Above
Grand Hotel Salome (Mexico City), Milan Furniture Fair, 2002
Arad designed the bedroom of a fictional urban hotel he invented, located in Mexico City. A circular bed complete with orbital/nesting 'furniture' (bed head, bedside table and desk) was positioned inside an inverted 'pill box' billboard made of curved acrylic panels clad in Lumisty™ film. This functioned as a 360° projection device displaying a wide range of images, information and links to live transmissions, and could be used for video conferencing or to create a more leisurely totally ambient environment. The bathroom mirror (top), was convertible from transparent to translucent or to opaque, allowing information and entertainment to be viewed from the bathroom.

Arad drew the potential boundlessness of IT into a down-to-earth union with comfort in this womb-like space. The central omnidirectional projection device in the form of a drum displayed a myriad of information. From the comfort of one's bed, city maps, messages, travel data, audio poems and multichannel entertainment, taking the viewer right into the middle of the football pitch, can be part of the immersive hotel-dwelling experience.

towards gadgets and new technologies, interactive conditions and new materials', a designer who is 'interested in these things as a part of a necessary kit of devices – as many and as diverse as may be necessary'.[3]

Both Lolita and Lo-rez-dolores-tabula-rasa are potentially semipermanent pieces. One of Arad's more hybrid interactive projects in the same mould is Grand Hotel Salome,[4] a speculative urban hotel located in Mexico City exhibited in Milan in 2002. A circular bed sat at the centre of an inverted 'pill box' billboard made of curved acrylic panels clad in Lumisty™ film, inside a shell that was entirely made of a screen onto which images were projected. It reflected Arad's desire to make a more synergistic relationship

between technology and tactile space. 'IT knows no boundaries: it is not limited to a small screen, keyboard or telephone,' he says. At the same time, what is important to him in a hotel is not 'someone else's idea of chic, but comfort and ease of access to information, entertainment and ambience'.

Arad drew the potential boundlessness of IT into a down-to-earth union with comfort in this womb-like space. The central omnidirectional projection device in the form of a drum displayed a myriad of information. From the comfort of one's bed, city maps, messages, travel data, audio poems and multichannel entertainment, taking the viewer right into the middle of the football pitch, were part of the immersive hotel-dwelling experience. Links to other live transmissions and video conferences, or even just scenes of visitors buzzing the room from the lobby, could be zapped into a media art gallery. The space functioned on cue as a total ambient environment. Arad gave his conception a localised virtual transparency. Outside the pill box, images in reverse could be seen, and in the bathroom the mirror was convertible from transparent to translucent or opaque, allowing information and entertainment to be viewed from here as well. 'When we do a project like this, we make sure it leaves the virtual world, and can be made like this,' says Arad.

One of Arad's housing designs is the living room and family dining room of the Millennium House (2002–)[5] in Doha, Qatar, a villa designed by Arata Isozaki for the

Top, middle and bottom
Grand Hotel Salome (Mexico City), Milan Furniture Fair, 2002
The drum-shaped omnidirectional projection wall. In the exhibition, visitors could view all of the projected images from outside the pillbox correctly, and the reversed images from the outside.

Above
**Living room and dining room,
Millennium House, Doha,
Qatar, 2002–**
A playful and extrovert design for
a villa designed by Arata Isozaki
for the minister of culture, with
different spaces designed by
various architects including
Achille Castiglioni and Ettore
Sottsass, and artists David
Hockney and Anish Kapoor. Arad
was commissioned to design the
living room, and the adjoining
family dining room, which was an
amphitheatre-style pit with a
horseshoe-shaped table the
server could walk into the middle
of, and transparent seats that
could be moved around its edge.

minister of culture. The house is made up of
many parts, each designed by different
architects, including Achille Castiglioni (gym),
David Hockney (swimming pool), and Ettore
Sottsass (formal reception), with set pieces by
artists such as Anish Kapoor. Arad's suite of
rooms features a programmable floor that can
be instructed to move in a certain pattern or
frozen into a given 'landscape'. The bedrooms
overlook this void, which moves like a pixel
board. An extrovert conception, it includes
lighting systems – full colour LEDs – made of
spheres that can be located anywhere in space
at any chosen size or colour, and operated by
remote control. The dining room is a space
shaped like the pit of an amphitheatre, with
transparent seats that move freely around, and

All these installations are
relatively low-res, or
on demand, rather than
high-res or pervasive.
Talking of the way things
operate in the interactive
business, Arad observes
that 'we are always fighting
to increase the resolution,
but sometimes you discover
the beauty of low-res'.

a horseshoe-shaped table the server can walk into the centre of. The design was featured in the 8th Venice Architecture Biennale in 2002, with a touchscreen so that visitors could design permutations of the floor themselves.

All these installations are relatively low-res, or on demand, rather than high-res or pervasive. Talking of the way things operate in the interactive business, Arad observes that 'we are always fighting to increase the resolution, but sometimes you discover the beauty of low-res'. He also dislikes talking about interactivity as something necessarily involving technology. 'It's a lazy word. I don't like it being overused, as if it is a compensation. Not everything has to be interactive. There has always been a relationship between design and technology. Now we can do certain things, and every medium can be translated to another medium.'

Arad also dislikes talking about interactivity as something necessarily involving technology. 'It's a lazy word. I don't like it being overused, as if it is a compensation. Not everything has to be interactive. There has always been a relationship between design and technology. Now we can do certain things, and every medium can be translated to another medium.'

Notes
1 Commissioned by the Gallery
Mourmans. Project team: Ron
Arad, Egon Hansen, Sebastien
Noel, Marcus Hirst, Helena
Ambrosio, The Gallery
Mourmans, Frero Tech bv, The
Light Surgeons (installation
film). Technical input: Massimo
Fucci, DuPont Surfaces, A & D
Relations, Créa Diffusion.
2 Design: Ron Arad. Produced
by: Moritz Waldemeyer for
Swarovski.
3 Peter Cook, *Nine Positions*,
British Pavilion exhibition
catalogue, 9th Venice
Architecture Biennale, The
British Council (London), 2004.
4 Design team: Ron Arad, Asa
Bruno. Video: The Light
Surgeons.
5 Design, modelling, imaging
and animation: Ron Arad
Associates, Geoff Crowther,
Egon Hansen and Paul
Gibbons.

The power of the spatial works Arad has crafted in recent years has to do with triggers – above all, sound, light and smell – for emotional surprise, and low-res solutions are showing themselves to be the ideal mediators for this emergent process.

Arad is as research-driven as he is committed to design at every single scale. His tempered-steel 'rolling shelves' he calls interactive, in that they are highly pliable: 'In the old days, I always used to bounce things, before I knew what to do with them.' The floor of the Millennium House can be interactive, or not, as desired.

The interactive facility of Arad's architecture is far from being gratuitous. He is currently designing the Upperworld hotel that will sit suspended on a bridge on the roof of Battersea Power Station, with a horizontal shuttle taking visitors to the door of their bedrooms. All the roofs will be convertible, so visitors can open up their bathrooms to the elements.

The power of the spatial works Arad has crafted in recent years has to do with triggers – above all, sound, light and smell – for emotional surprise, and low-res solutions are showing themselves to be the ideal mediators for this emergent process. ⌁

Interactive Urban Design As Event: Christian Moeller

Once a practising architect, engaged in the offices of Günter Behnisch, Christian Moeller was attracted away from the conventional route of the profession by the stimulation and opportunities of the 1980s multimedia art scene. In this profile by **Lucy Bullivant**, the now professor of media arts/design at UCLA describes his aptitude for the accessible, and why he prefers 'temporary fireworks' and experiment in his interactive practice over permanent installations.

Above right
Do Not Touch, Energy Gallery, Science Museum, London, 2004
Children as well as adults are invited to walk on a circular carpet of rubber and touch a 6-metre-high pole, which gives them a mild electric shock. The frisson of entering a no-go area, and the energy exchange received, made them think about energy by feeling it.

In the summer of 2003, an interactive installation about the frisson of transgressive activities was unveiled in London at the Science Museum's new permanent interactive Energy Gallery. Called Do Not Touch, it is intended for children as much as for adults. A titillating play on permission and choice, transforming the phenomenon of energy into direct physical experience, it consists of a circular carpet of rubber admonishing 'DO NOT TOUCH', with a 6-metre-high pole in the middle.

The work of the German interactive architect Christian Moeller, the installation is now on permanent display, and sets up a 'danger zone' of experience that is rare for museum displays, and particularly so for one aimed at an audience predominantly of children.[1] Visitors entering this

space hear an acoustically amplified warning sound and, if they touch the pole, receive a mild electric shock. As curator of the gallery Hannah Redler says: 'Visitors can decide for themselves whether they feel this is a punishment or a reward.'

This was not the first time Moeller had made a piece for the Science Museum's Digital Visions areas. In 2000 he adapted special-effects technology to create Particles, a swarm of glowing, animated particles projected on a screen, creating a silhouette of the visitor in motion. Insound Out, a second piece the same year, this time for the museum's Digital Sounds area, allows visitors to experiment with electronic sound. Standing on two vibrating steel grids, they can physically experience the ways in which digital technology can generate sound through a camera motion recognition system and a pair of parabolic sound projectors that enable sound to be focused at very specific points in the space. Sound elements are therefore composed by the movements of the visitor in front of the video camera, and then played into his or her body.

The Children's Gallery at the Science Museum was one of the first interactive spaces in a UK museum, making Moeller's contributions part of a long tradition of pioneering curatorial work there.

'My interest and opportunities came from the media art scene,' says Moeller. Previously a practising architect, he increasingly realised that his biggest challenges lay in developing works with electronic media. 'Architecture is a great profession but it is hard to accomplish great works in the field. If Hollywood had to make movies under architecture's circumstances, they would have closed down the industry by now. I wanted to work with a bigger variety of people, not necessarily a decision to do with interdisciplinarity.'

Moeller's introduction to the media scene came via Peter Weibel, the director of Frankfurt's Institute for New Media, who had a very strong affinity to architecture. 'The Institute was the most challenging place on earth,' Moeller continues. 'I was fascinated by the sheer existence of it. It was not about wanting to change things but about what I wanted to do.' His works often show a wry sense of humour, and their clarity gives them a certain functional beauty: 'I like a certain irony a lot, and I like beauty, but I don't call my works beautiful.'

In the late 1980s Moeller set about copying the technological facilities Weibel had set up at the institute, and became the first architect to have his own electronic media studio within an architectural studio. As his media architecture works[2] took off in the early 1990s, he gradually phased out the more conventional architectural commissions: 'I didn't want to use CAD to design buildings, but real-time phenomena. It was a transition, not a cut.' His staff included former students, but also, and necessarily, collaborators who were experts within the field of art media, or musicians. However, 'I never mixed up academic with professional work', he says, pointing out that one of his current assistants is a former doctor.

At the time, CAD was yet to be taken up by architecture, and desktop publishing was yet to make digital media activities affordable. For example, a real-time video digitising system cost $90,000, far more than the comparative costs of the desktop systems used for interactive design

today. 'Now you can buy an Apple notebook with everything. My 10-year-old daughter edits her own videos,' says Moeller.

Rather than working on permanent pieces, as 'permanent work reduces the ability to make very strong experiments', Moeller prefers 'temporary fireworks'. With the exception of the Science Museum installations, the overwhelming majority of his projects are short term in duration. His work has consistently used electronic media to create architecture based on the idea of dialogue within the urban context. He harnesses sound, light, weather conditions, movements of the body and human emotions to create spaces that are responsive and manipulable, as well as clearly defined: 'I like things that are accessible – not providing lots of content to explore.' It is hard to imagine the maker of works intended to unleash innovative, unfolding relationships between people and the spaces they inhabit being satisfied with more formal and tectonic construction processes and materials. 'I originally called myself an architect, but I am not one any more,' he says.

Much of his early work included collaborations with bodies in Frankfurt. For the Teater am Turm (TAT) in the city, Moeller set up a cinematoscope in a subway station, and a kinetic light sculpture for a developer on the facade of a shopping mall. He also made an image- and sensor-based piece enabling the viewer to travel from skyscrapers to the homeless communities of the city, set in the Carmelite Monastery. There were installations in spaces outside the hermetic white box of the gallery, for instance in the former subway tunnel at Unter den Linden in Berlin, or the Saint Roche assembly building in Brussels. Meanwhile, he showed virtual architecture pieces such as Algorithmic Habitat at a media art exhibition by Peter Weibel at Galerie Tanja Grunert in Cologne, Germany, and Space (Im)balance in the Danube Park in Linz, Austria.

Performance has been a vector of Moeller's work, and Electro Clips, realised in 1994 with the support of

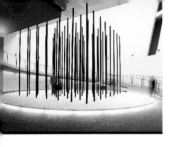

Top
Audio Grove, Aoyama Spiral Gallery, Tokyo, 1997
The Audio Grove sound installation was commissioned by the Spiral Gallery in Aoyama, Tokyo (designed by Fumihiko Maki) in 1997, and staged that year. A forest of iron poles linked to touch-sensitive electronic sensors triggered an audio and light system.

the TAT Frankfurt and the Ars Electronica Festival in Linz, Austria, was an experimental dance piece with sound elements by electronic music composer Pete Namlook. 'The idea was to have the dancer produce all the sounds, his movement creating the entire musical event,' explains Moeller. 'The dancer would become the conductor of a virtual orchestra whose instruments he activated by his movements in and through light projections.' Stephen Galloway, the lead dancer in William Forsythe's Ballet Frankfurt, was ideal because he had the skills to 'respond to a set of possibilities rather than a composed score with a fixed choreography'. Together with lighting director Louis Philippe Demers, Moeller designed the interactivity by measuring changes in light and

first at the TAT in Frankfurt, and later at the Tochoji Monastery in Shinjuku (in conjunction with the Japanese curators ARTLAB-Prospect 2), in Tokyo, in 1997. The installation used the mechanical floor employed in Space (Im)balance, to which Moeller attached laser scanners projecting a virtual floor into the stage space. The visitor would walk across a ramp to the movable platform.

In the monastic temple of Tochoji, a very beautiful and meditative place, there is a cemetery where the monks put stones engraved with the names of people into a pool of water. Beneath this pool, Moeller created an artificial lake of light generated by two argon lasers that shifted with the visitor's position on the balance platform. As the gradient of the artificial light surface changed, the movement triggered a particle system invisible to the visitor and moved around the room like an audio cluster that he or she could hear but not see, derived from a tape of insects under water. Its movement was the result of a gravitational algorithm. In interplay with the sloping virtual floor, the particle swarm moved around with increasing noise like mosquitos, particularly when it came close to the visitor on the platform.

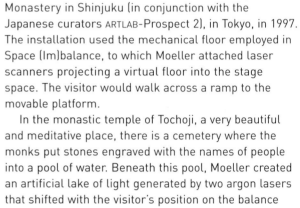

Audio Grove was one of three sound installations commissioned by the Aoyama Spiral Gallery/Wacoal Art Centre in Tokyo (the building designed by Fumihiko Maki) staged in 1997. Here, 64 upright iron poles of almost 6 metres were linked to touch-sensitive electronic sensors which, when touched, emitted sounds by triggering an audio system. A simple touch activated one sound, and the simultaneous touch of two poles moved the overall audio up or down by one octave.

The composer Ludger Brümmer used a physical modelling system to create the most resonant sound elements for Audio Grove. 'He engineers virtual objects as instruments (on computer), locates them in a mathematically constructed virtual world and designs the attack to create a particular sound,' explains Moeller. The installation's touch-sensitivity was also harnessed to light for the installation, with 25 spotlights aligned into place. When the poles were touched, the lights went on and off alternately, generating what Moeller calls 'a light shadow texture' on the floor, like a carpet. 'It became a big meeting point, with people having fun, and causing effects with the light sensors' – very atmospheric at night below a huge skylight. However, a side effect the team were not prepared for was the impact of such large crowds of people wanting to touch the poles at the same time. Their enthusiasm unfortunately had the unintentional effect of corrupting the sound quality of the performance on the opening night ('in an open space, you are going to lose these spatial effects'), so Moeller and his collaborators quickly made a one-page photocopy 'user manual' which stopped people

Above
Virtual Cage, TAT Frankfurt, 1993, and Tochoji Monastery, Shinjuku, Tokyo, 1997
Bathed in soft light from lasers, the visitor stood on a glass-surface platform that tilted with his or her movements. These, and the shift in rays of light, in turn triggered an 'insect swarm' – recordings of insects under water – to move through the room, creating an eerie sense of being wrapped in sound and light.

shade on the floor of the stage whenever Galloway moved in the spotlights. Tiny light sensors (photo transistors) were distributed around the floor, and at the back of the stage were metal rods with light sensors. 'The dancer is then literally inside a musical instrument, moving in a kind of ambient piano, as the beams of the stage spotlights become "strings" that produce sounds when touched.' The installation was shown repeatedly on MTV, and a CD, 'Music for Ballet', sold out immediately.

The exploratory piece that led him to conclude that site-specific art could not exist as an autonomous pursuit, Virtual Cage, one of a number of sound pieces, was realised in 1993,

Camera Music/Kinetic Shadows, Aoyama Spiral Gallery, 1997
Abstract kinetic representations of people in the gallery lobby were captured by video camera and rear-projected onto a screen. When they saw their bodies reflected as sparkling clusters of dynamic pixel rods on the projection screen, the visitors reacted spontaneously. Their gesticulations caused passers-by in the street, who could glimpse them making this response but not the digital clusters in motion through the glass facade, to join in.

Kinetic Light Sculpture, Zeilgalerie, Frankfurt, 1992
This was the first time a light installation of this kind had been installed on the facade of a building, on a new shopping mall in central Frankfurt. Mobile blue-yellow clusters of light changed patterns in response to the prevailing weather and temperature conditions.

touching the poles with both hands and immediately restored the quality of the installation's sound effects.

A second work for the already atmospheric Spiral Gallery building playfully induced physical movement on the part of its onlookers. In Camera Music/Kinetic Shadows, Moeller provoked visitors in the lobby into spontaneous and often very amusing-looking actions by reflecting them as sparkling clusters of dynamic pixel rods on a rear projection screen. As the visitors quickly figured out that their movements created a synchronous effect on their personal 'cluster', they began to wave their arms, stride up and down, dance or wiggle about. Passers-by outside in the street could also see these freeform gesticulations (though not the digital imagery) through the glass facade, which made them want to immediately go inside to find out what all the fuss was about.

The digital shadow concept behind the work is echoed by Particles, Moeller's 2000 installation for the Science Museum's Energy Gallery. It also shares a common impulse with Klein Dytham Architects and Toshi Iwai's ICE installation at the Bloomberg headquarters, created six years later (see pages 12–13), although ICE reveals both participants and the vivid chromatic digital movement flows to passers-by, rather than setting up a concealed effect to the street. Moeller says: 'I'm trying to make works that people can react to without much information. Here, after people have had their sensation, they can move on.'

An important project from the early stages of Moeller's work with electronic media is the Kinetic Light Sculpture (1992). At the time, Space (Im)balance was nearing completion, and a visitor coming to Moeller's studio to view it, architect Rüdiger Kramm, mentioned that he was looking for a concept for a light installation on the facade of the Zeilgalerie, a new mall in central Frankfurt. The project was Moeller's biggest commission so far, and functioned only from twilight onwards. The facade was covered with a layer of perforated sheet metal, and as dusk fell it transformed itself into moving blue-yellow clusters of light, their patterns changing according to the current weather conditions, like a chameleon. A total of 120 halogen spotlights, in three groups and mounted on catwalks, beamed from behind the metal sheet, triggered on by twilight and then off again by dawn. Each spotlight had a movable lid that could be computer controlled to vary the light tones. At 0°C, the wall was monochrome blue, but as the

temperature increased, yellow clusters would form. The direction of the wind monitored by the weather station on the roof caused the temperature-controlled colours to move across the wall.

Near the top of the building a 3 x 16 metre LED display screen was installed showing the oscillating graphic renderings of the ambient sounds in the street. This had the appearance of a white line moving like an oscillograph to the sounds of the passers-by, possibly the first of its kind ever built, and by day it operated as a news board – the first interactive facade installation of this size. The building, unused by night, created a huge exodus of viewers by day.

The Bitwalls in Elbe and Bielefeld in Germany (2002) were the culminations of Moeller's longstanding efforts to create systems for facades that would function both as an architectonic surface and as an image carrier, during the day and at night. For this he developed mechanical pixels that could switch from black to white quickly and inexpensively. In addition, he saw a number of problems with existing LED display surfaces: firstly, they are placed without any consideration to architectural logic, and the dimensions are too small for viewer satisfaction. They also look an ugly blackish-grey when switched off, but, in fact, due to their commercial role, they have to be constantly on. He imagined a surface on which, for days or weeks, nothing happens, and then when something very relevant to be communicated crops up, it is immediately transformed into a display. Moeller envisaged the cost as being similar to that of a curtain-wall facade system, which reduced the possible complexity of the display. The piece was feasible transmitting only bit-map depictions, and working with low resolutions with pixel sizes of up to 30 x 30 centimetres, not unlike German architects realities:united's BIX Matrix system for the Kunsthaus in Graz, completed in 2003 (see pages 82–5). Various experiments with mechanical pixels for use as dynamic

graphics on building surfaces produced 'walking figures' made up of very large pixels, yet no less expressive for their grainy quality.

For Elbe, Moeller made a 10-metre-high display pillar on which the banks of the Elbe River literally unfold in 800 kilometres of digital film footage, an installation placed in a real backdrop next to a road on the outskirts of the city. It uses an electromagnetic hinged pixel, which has a permanent magnet embedded into the hinge that swings on its vertical axis. The project in Bielefeld, for a hotel and trade-fair complex was curtailed by the bankruptcy of the investor, but in its creative planning Moeller focused on the south-facing entrance wall, creating a 'virtual stretching' effect, an image matrix interrupted at regular intervals to enlarge the surface without spending more money. This would have increased the physical display dimensions by interweaving empty spaces into the moving image.

The Bielefeld installation was cancelled by the

client due to lack of funds; a few other of Moeller's projects have also not advanced, but generally he has been extremely lucky in finding clients with the passion and money to back him. However, he is not creating from a tabula rasa: 'The constraints are created by the client and his context. It usually helps to find the client's topic: until then I'm like a white page.'

In Los Angeles, there are few designers doing what Moeller is doing, which is ironic considering the proximity of Silicon Valley, and indeed the special-effects industry attached to Hollywood. Cheese, a work from 2003 that takes its cue from the 'weird social world of the entertainment industry where performed friendliness is part of the currency', is Moeller's

Above
Bitwalls, designed for Elbe and Bielefeld, Germany, 2002
These systems for public urban facades function as an architectonic surface and as an image carrier by day and at night. The banks of the Elbe literally unfold in a crude pixel on the pillar next to a road on the outskirts of the city.

Right and below
Various experiments with mechanical pixels for use as dynamic graphics on building surfaces.

Notes
1 The work raised liability and safety issues, and the Science Museum undertook a full technical report before satisfying itself that it was safe to proceed with the installation.
2 Moeller's work is chronicled in a first-person account, *A Time and Place: Christian Moeller Media Architecture 1991–2003*, Lars Müller (Baden, Switzerland), 2004, and is also on his website, www.christian-moeller.com.

interpretation of this social context. A commission from the Center for Neuromorphic Systems Engineering at the California Institute of Technology and the Williamson Gallery Art Center College of Design in Pasadena, Cheese was a human–computer interaction scenario. Six actresses were filmed on video, with the instruction to hold a fixed smile for as long as possible. The computer's perception system scrutinised the results, and whenever their faces began to fall – even just by a twitch of a muscle – an irritating alarm beeped, alerting the individual to show more 'sincerity'. A sequence of flat-panel monitors showed the 'emotion recognition' exercise as alternating fake smiles and the melancholy unease of the performers recovering in the intervening breaks to an aural backdrop of alert signals. Visitors to the resulting exhibition could see the fluctuations in attained levels of 'sincerity' on a vertical bar, switching from red to green. Cheese clearly went behind the curtain of human responsiveness, while Do Not Touch simply tugged playfully at it.

Cheese was incongruous in Hollywood, and media art/architecture is present only within certain protocols in the us, with Diller & Scofidio, Asymptote and a few others representing the exception. Moeller feels that his field of interactive media space installations is much more of a European and Japanese phenomenon – the Netherlands, Germany and the UK are very strong, and the Japanese are 'great in media design'. Many trips to Japan to install pieces have given him the chance to observe media art characterised by a sense of beauty and adherence to minimalism, but also affected by changes in social restrictions leading to trailblazing work by Toshio Iwai and Masahi Fujihata, not forgetting Toyo Ito's Tower of Winds in Yokohama, built in 1993. The tower's kaleidoscope of colour and light is created by the floodlights surrounding it, representing the visual complexity of Tokyo as a never-ceasing, ever-changing wind. At the time, Ito said he wanted to design architecture like an 'unstable flowing body'; Moeller feels it is 'beautiful without being too expressive'. Too expressive? 'Yes, architecture is a pretty permanent installation, and if it gets too expressive it becomes like stage design – you get bored of it.' ∆

D-Tower, NOX

Doetinchem, the Netherlands, 1998–2004

Right
The bulbous, vegetal form of D-tower's prefabricated epoxy structure. Every evening it is transformed by coloured light. Depending on the results of a questionnaire completed by locals on D-tower's website about their feelings, it can turn blue for happiness, red for love, green for hate or yellow for fear.

Conducting your love life or expressing your innermost feelings through an architectural medium, one that seemingly replaces the traditional village green where people met up and shared experiences, is a pretty far-reaching social proposition. But D-tower, a collaboration between architect Lars Spuybroek of NOX in Rotterdam, and QS Serafijn, a Rotterdam-based artist, aims to do just that, writes **Lucy Bullivant**, in a way that transcends any notion of a pure prosthetic device with an architectural system of communication.

One evening last September, D-tower[1] was opened in front of a huge crowd in the city of Doetinchem, in the eastern Netherlands. It is a permanent public art work with its own website. NOX's[2] tower looks zoomorphic, a little like a pony's legs. Its website (www.d-toren.nl), which being handwritten has an air of intimacy about it, maps the emotions of Doetinchem's inhabitants in response to a questionnaire created by artist QS Serafijn, determining the intensity of their feelings of love, hate, happiness and fear.

The tower then abstracts the emotions of these answers to the questions through its use of colour, transmitting 'the State of the Town' each evening, assuming the colour of the most intensely felt emotion. After running for a month, the architects concluded that it had been often blue (for happiness) or red (for love) and sometimes green (for hate), but NOX's Lars Spuybroek reports that it has not yet been yellow (for fear).

Every six months, a different group of 50 of the city's inhabitants will complete further editions of the questionnaire. Questions become more and more precise, and the answers are then translated into the form of different 'landscapes' shown on the website. Spuybroek explains that in the process, all the ins and outs of their emotional lives are made visible, including ongoing discussions about hot issues. The response to an initial newspaper advert, and

via the website, for 50 volunteers far exceeded the number of people required, so the first group was selected according to age, sex and neighbourhood, to make it as representative as possible.

The tall, prefabricated epoxy structure, which Spuybroek likens to a Gothic vault because the columns and surface share the same continuum, provokes attention in its different guises by day and night. Each evening, the D-tower light comes on simultaneously with the street lighting, and onlookers can also check the colour of the tower on a webcam at www.d-toren.nl/webcam.

'D-tower is a coherent hybrid of different media, where architecture is part of a larger interactive system of relationships,' says Spuybroek. 'It is a project where the intensive (feelings, qualities) and the extensive (space, quantities) start exchanging roles, where human action, colour, money, value, feelings all become networked entities.' The city's residents can also place their personal messages concerning the 'landscapes' shown on the site in a capsule underneath the tower.

Creating a connection between all these elements, D-tower also sends prewritten love letters and flowers from and to designated addresses. At the end of each year it will present a prize of 10,000 euros to the address in the city that, as a result of the website computing, scores the highest level of emotions.

> The tall, prefabricated epoxy structure, which Spuybroek likens to a Gothic vault because the columns and surface share the same continuum, provokes attention in its different guises by day and night.

Top and bottom
Visualisations of D-tower in Doetinchem, lit up at night, and at twilight just before its lighting is switched on.

Notes
1 Project team: NOX (Lars Spuybroek with Pitupong Chaowakul, Chris Seung-woo Yoo and Norbert Palz), QS Serafijn and the V2_Lab (Simon de Bakker and Artem Baguinski).
2 www.noxarch.com.

Son-O-House, NOX
Son en Breugel, the Netherlands, 2000–04

Lars Spuybroek of NOX has also recently made a public artwork for Industrieschap Ekkersrijt, in collaboration with composer Edwin van der Heide. Here, Lucy Bullivant describes a project that builds a 'memoryscape' of sounds in and near the space visitors participate in making.

Above
The metal beam structure, intended for meetings and general relaxation, at night. Its design is based on choreographed sets of visitors' movements inscribed on paper bands as cuts, while a sound piece activated by sensors registers these movements. Through van der Heide's programming, new sound patterns are continually evolved as a 'memoryscape'.

Son-O-House,[1] 'a house where sounds live', is, as NOX's Lars Spuybroek explains, not a real house but a structure that refers to the bodily movements of visitors, and a sound work continuously generating new sound patterns activated by sensors picking up these movements. Situated on the highway between Son en Breugel and Eindhoven, in the IT and new media zone of an industrial park, it functions as a statement about new technology and social space where people can hold meetings or come to relax and enjoy the ambience.

The metal beam structure itself is based on choreographed sets of human movements inscribed on paper bands as cuts. This formula created 'an arabesque of complex intertwining lines', and Spuybroek then married the open structure of lines with the closed surface of the ground to create a three-dimensional porous structure like interlacing vaults that lean on each other, or sometimes cut into each other.

To make the 3,300-square-metre structure function as an interactive sound work, 23 sensors positioned at strategic points indirectly influence the music emitted. People can not just hear sound in a musical structure, but also participate in the composition of the sound. 'It is an instrument, score and studio at the same time,' says Spuybroek. The system of sounds, composed and programmed by sound artist Edwin van der Heide,[2] is based on moiré effects of interference of closely related frequencies. 'The visitor does not influence the sound directly, which is so often the case with interactive art,' continues Spuybroek. 'One influences the real-time composition itself that generates the sounds. The score is an evolutionary memoryscape that develops with the traced behaviour of the actual bodies in the space.'

The sound work is continuous, with endless variations, none of which are scored but derive from bodily intervention in the space. One visitor commented that he could hear the installation humming on his approach to the house by bike, like the sound of birds in the background. As he entered the space, the sounds changed, and he could feel that it was his presence and movements that were the cause of this. The concept is a potent one, premised on a hybrid, directly body-driven architecture that is a relatively unexplored area, and Spuybroek needs to be given the opportunity to develop these ideas further in other locations. ∆

Top and bottom
The winding internal space of the structure encourages visitors to linger. NOX has placed sensors here that indirectly influence the sounds it emits by picking up on the sounds visitors make entering or moving around. Sounds alter as a result, and an ongoing compositional loop is created, reflected in the building's appearance.

Note
1 NOX project team: Lars Spuybroek with Chris Seung-woo Yoo, Josef Glas, Ludovica Tramontin, Kris Mun, Geri Stavreva and Nicola Lammers.
2 www.erdh.net.

Mediating Devices for a Social Statement:

Tobi Schneidler

Interactive Architect

German architect Tobi Schneidler, with his team at the Smart Studio of the Interactive Institute in Stockholm, Sweden, integrates interactive media and network technologies within spatial environments. Here, he explains to **Lucy Bullivant** how, for him, information technology is not merely hardware or software, but an essential tool that can create 'mediating devices for a social statement'.

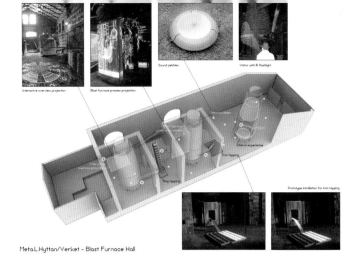

Meta.L.Hyttan/Verket – Blast Furnace Hall

Top left
Top left
Smart Studio and servo architects, Responsive Fields, exhibited at 'Latent Utopias', Graz, Austria, 2002–03 and 'Algorithmic Revolution', ZKM, Karlsruhe, 2004
A seemingly elastic structure of lattice-shaped sensory light modules incorporating digital 'agents' responded to visitors' movements, triggering changing patterns of light.

Clockwise, from top right
Meta L Hyttan, Avesta, Sweden, 2002
For Avesta, one of the birthplaces of the Swedish steel industry, Smart Studio, led by Schneidler and commissioned by the town council's cultural department, proposed the transformation of a historic blast-furnace hall into an interactive environment where visitors could learn and experience history, science and art.
1 Model and overview of the layout of the blast-furnace hall.
2 Floor of the hall with guided floor projection, an illuminated time line and 'hotspot' that worked a bit like a hyperlink on a web page, but here as part of the physical page. Instead of touchscreens and audio guides, each part of the hall had a customised design equipping it with sound, light, visuals and kinetic devices that responded to visitors' preferences.
3 Visitors were given a handheld torch for exploring the dark space of the hall. It was designed to trigger information and effects, and could be programmed to operate in specific ways for particular visitors, helping to personalise their experience.
4 Interactive digital model of Avesta made for Smart Studio's presentation to the client, Avesta town council's cultural department.

Tobi Schneidler is an architect who fuses digital media and physical space. He sees interactive media and network technologies as key ingredients in a new design, thinking about connected, real-world spaces. A German-born Architectural Association graduate, he directs projects at the Smart Studio of the Interactive Institute in Stockholm, a multidisciplinary research institute specialising in digital media.[1] The Smart Studio[2] creates tangible media expressions from a mix of art, technology and science in the form of interdisciplinary projects generating new questions and reflections. These are disseminated mainly as international exhibitions, though some permanent and provocative installations have already been made as, under Schneidler's leadership, the technocratic vision is supplanted by one that is culturally and socially driven.

'The design question is not one of shaping the increasingly ubiquitous technology in itself. Far more important is how these emerging possibilities will inform new cultures of dwelling as well as social relationships, and thereby the

London   Berlin

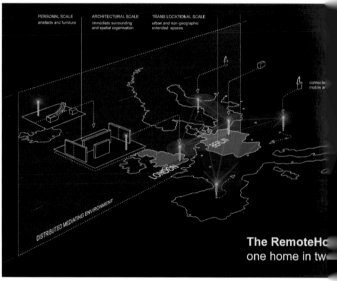

PERSONAL SCALE
artefacts and furniture

ARCHITECTURAL SCALE
immediate surrounding
and spatial organisation

TRANS LOCATIONAL SCALE
urban and non-geographic
extended spaces

LONDON

DISTRIBUTED MEDIATING ENVIRONMENT

The RemoteHo
one home in tw

Top left
RemoteHome, Science Museum, London, and Raumlabor, Berlin, May 2003
Two environments were styled as apartment rooms kitted out with furniture, one in London, the other in Berlin, and connected as real-time mediated environments. A 1:1 –1:10 version was included in 'Touching the Invisible', an exhibition with six Smart Studio projects, at the Ludwig Museum, Budapest, in 2004, touring to Moscow, London and Berlin (2005). The two RemoteHome spaces in London and Berlin were designed with matching elements, to relay tactile, evocative communication between the two via furniture and wall surfaces.

Top right
Scale diagram of the RemoteHome project showing its concept applied through a range of scales, from the personal level of artefacts and furniture, to an architectural scale of spatial organisations and, finally, to distributed translocational spaces.

Opposite, top left
The RemoteHome system diagram shows how the remote spaces with their interactive features and furniture were connected as a system.

Opposite, top right
The sensor and actuator wall. Movement and activities were picked up by ultrasonic sensors embedded in both spaces and translated into kinetic wave motions on the the walls of the apartments, one in each city. Their data is picked up by the system, driving the local feedback and remote effects.

Opposite, bottom
People in the London apartment made 'ambient scribbles' in an underlit bed of sand that could then be transmitted to the Berlin apartment, reappearing on a glowing ambient wall.

design of architecture to come,' says Schneidler. His team focuses on exploring interactivity and its impact on spatial environments, evaluating this theme through physical prototyping, because the relationships between physical features, media effects and the user are too complex to explore in a physical scale model. The prototyping allows the time-based and interactive effects on users to be assessed. 'The relationship has to be modelled in time and effect, Schneidler explains, 'rather than just as an aesthetic, scaled equivalent of the final anticipated outcome.'

The studio's project-based activities entail creating close-knit teams of specialists. 'In all the projects I am trying to position the group so we don't duplicate skills and can all participate in the decision-making, with the architectural or design part relating to the engineering skills, like an advertising art director and copywriter team,' says Schneidler, emphasising that 'even technology can be developed and implemented in a creative process, although it often goes against the learned culture of the engineering profession'.

One collaboration with an outside party was Responsive Fields (of Lattice Archipelogics, to give it its full name), a speculative architecture audiovisual installation first shown as part of the architectural exhibition 'Latent Utopias', in Graz, Austria, in 2002–03. The collaboration, between the Smart Studio Interactive Institute and servo architects, produced a structure of individual sensory light modules (in lattice forms) with digital 'agents' responding to the occupation and movements of visitors, triggering an adaptive and dynamic pattern of light (thereby creating the archipelogics). Moving luminous bodies were repelled or attracted by the visitor, and a responsive 3-D soundpiece located him or her in space, amplifying the experience.

'The very structure was hybrid,' says Schneidler. 'Its physical features and the spatial organisation corresponded to human scale and movement, while the intangible effects of light and audio intensified the time-based and interactive experience.'

Spatially mapped sensors and algorithmic processing established the logic that gave the installation its synaptic presence. The visitor became part of the installation, a mediated environment transcending a screen-based experience that challenged human presence and cognition. Schneidler says the interaction was deliberately ambiguous and suggestive, provoking 'a more intuitive experience'.

The broad-based specialisms of the Smart Studio include two architects, Adam Somlai-Fischer (see pages 97–8) and Pablo Miranda, as well as engineers and programmers. Besides Miranda, Frederick Petersson (in Swedish, a 'kreativ ingenjör') contributed to Responsive Fields 'design scenario thinking' – working out how to position the installation, what the algorithms should do, and how the light and interactive experience should work.

Schneidler's largest scale (realised work) project to date is Meta L Hyttan, a proposal at Avesta, in Sweden, converting Avesta Verket, a historic steel plant in the city, into an interactive visitor experience. Commissioned by the cultural department of Avesta city council, Meta L Hyttan is not merely a scenographic design, but shows how interactive technologies could be embedded in a real place, and information and effects accessed in different ways.

With effects hidden in the structure through the use of pervasive computing networks that cannot be seen, the idea of extending the space with personalised content is realised by giving visitors a special exploration tool – a standard torch – to activate them and record their journey. Visitors trigger interactive content as they explore the space, with the torch light acting as a basic pointing device. The media are not delivered through typical exhibition interfaces such as touchscreens or audio guides. Instead, each location is individually equipped with audio and light sources, visual projections and/or kinetic actuators. These channels are then 'digitally choreographed', as Schneidler puts it, to animate each area of interest, according to the personal preferences of the visitor.

The torch light works as an identifier, triggering different shows adaptively, explains Schneidler, meaning that 'the same physical place can effectively be coloured and reshaped in response to personal

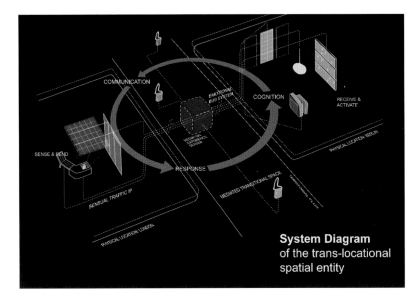

System Diagram
of the trans-locational
spatial entity

interaction'. This introduces a layered set of responses: 'Changing stories are told depending on the identity of the visitor.' The space is divided into distinct interactive zones, each marked with yellow rings as hotspots. When the visitor points the torch light at the hotspot, an invisible infrared signal travels from it to the hotspot. This identifies the visitor and his or her choice of lamp to the system in the background, which can then automatically trigger the various local media events linked to the zone. Schneidler explains that the underlying system uses standard network technology, running the same protocols that operate on office networks and the global Internet. Together with an adaptable software platform, developed by the Interactive Institute, this system becomes easily scalable and cost efficient.

The often-quoted phrase 'augmented reality' means the possibility of extending real-life environments with the help of interactive media and interfaces that link the physical space to digital information. Schneidler explains the implications of this: 'We can overlay interactive media with physical spaces, creating new environmental entities that challenge the perception of our world.' To achieve this, he maintains, one has to look at information technology not as a unit or device, but as an enabling structure that merges into the fabric of the space. Control signals, streamed media, sensors, output devices and computers are linked to that invisible system, but the effects inform a profound spatial relationship.

The important achievement of the Avesta project is that the interaction experience it gives is site specific, rather than media specific. 'The immediate qualities of the space are enhanced, and placed in an extended media context of adaptive content,' says Schneidler. 'The visitor is subject to a new duality of context and space. The absolute scale of the historic edifice and the dynamic scale of the digital media topology.'

The much discussed RemoteHome project, realised internationally as a public installation on a number of occasions in the last few years, evolved from Schneidler's 'personal ambitions for integrating a project with my own flat and life. It is not just a technology research project, but more a kind of autobiographical result of my life.' A communication system, it extends the idea of home as a private and situated space to one that connects homes in two different cities. The RemoteHome is an apartment that exists in two countries at the same time, its floor space distributed over two cities and stitched together by digital networks. It responds to changing cultures of living and the rise of distant relationships. Communications and media technologies including mobile phones and instant messaging are already creating new scenarios of sharing friendship and intimacy over long distances. With RemoteHome, Schneidler asks the question: What will happen if real-time mediated communication were to become part of our everyday environment, the spaces we inhabit, the furniture we use and the items we cherish?

Sensory furniture and fittings detect and distribute impressions rather than information about the inhabitants. These cues of occupation are then transmitted via the Internet to the respective other side, where they surface through kinetic, tangible features and light installations – 'tactile and visual cues on furniture and other physical

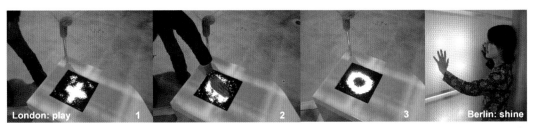

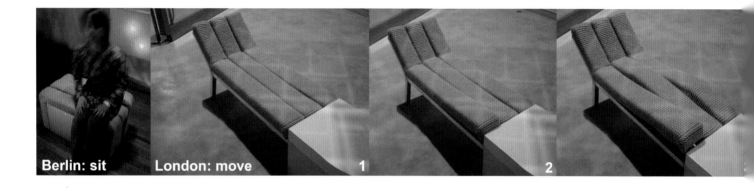

Berlin: sit   London: move   1   2

surfaces'. This way, Schneidler explains, 'the home stretches beyond borders, and helps friends to stay in touch, literally, through tangible and sensual communication', an emotional and intuitive form of presence.

Model apartments were set up at the Science Museum in London and at the Raumlabor in Berlin, and distant audiences were allowed to participate and interact with each other in real time. In London an interactive lounge table was suspended from the ceiling. When someone drew on or moved it, the surface became animated, triggering ambient music on a wall of lights in the Berlin apartment, a sound shaft, suspended over an inflatable couch. Inhabitants of this space could in turn reply with spoken messages by grabbing the sound shaft and moving it over a table. Small light sensors picked up the movement of a light beam travelling over the sensor field, relaying it to the table in London.

'There are some remote presence projects at MIT and elsewhere, but lots are focused on the personal device; for instance, a stone that heats up and conveys presence. You don't need to show the visible technology. The simplest projects are the best,' says Schneidler.

'It's very important for me,' he adds, 'that the project is not about interactive technology or smart space per se, but about creating environments that act as mediating devices for a social statement.' And it is because Schneidler is motivated in this way that he has defined a matrix of categories with which he works, with three levels and three forms of application. The levels are personal, architectural and translocational, and the applications process-based: concept, interactive prototype stage and, thirdly, real-world commissions. 'I'm very interested in defining this as an architectural Bauhaus concept, in the sense of scaling up from a door handle to an urban space. I want to do an equivalent.'

Uniquely, RemoteHome embodies all three levels. This space of its architecture stretches the conventions of physical scale, extending one environment to different locations. Schneidler argues that, here, spatial coherence is no longer expressed through physical enclosure, but 'topologies of social relations'. These can be lived through the digital network architecture. Local can mean 'personal loci', rather than just a static, geographic point of reference. The prospect of addressing the environment as an embodied home, ephemeral, scalable and mobile, motivates him greatly.

Schneidler suggests that the relationship with our environments and the artefacts we handle is increasingly changing towards the intangible: correspondence is going digital; travel receipts are mere electronic tags; money is becoming virtual. The effects of mobile communication are transforming our experience of location and geographical distance, establishing what he calls parallel worlds of experience. Subsequently, the effects are also triggering changes in the individual's notion of personal context, or personal space, now as digital as it is physical.

He is interested in how people react to new technological and social conditions, for, as he says: 'Many changes have happened in a very rapid way.' In the new field of interaction design, the service design experience has become important, and new thinking is flooding the mainstream. One example Schneidler loves, because it tries to keep things very simple, is the I-Pod, a mobile resource for playing music, simultaneously connecting the wearer with an online, virtual music store.

The ReFashion Lab (2001)[3] extends the reach of a fashion studio Schneidler's sister Stefanie set up in Berlin, as an exhibition installation presenting into a unique form of interactive boutique space, using it as an experimental platform to 'test new scenarios of interaction between people, space and media'. One of the Smart Studio's more collaborative projects, contributors included: Nokia Research (Finland); Tomato Interactive (UK); Scanner, alias Robin Rimbaud, the British digital-sound artist; Christiane Posch, an Austrian industrial and interaction designer; as well as

Above
RemoteHome, Science Museum, London, and Raumlabor, Berlin, May 2003, and e-culture fair, Amsterdam, October 2003
The Busy Bench is a piece of furniture designed to tease the distant flatmate. Occupying it in one of the apartments transforms the corresponding bench in the other apartment into an animated object, seemingly with a mind of its own.

Above
ReFashion Lab, Moderna Museet and Liljewalchs Konsthall, Stockholm, 2001
An interactive boutique space including various elements designed by different team members, from a personalised mirror to interactive walls and elements. The ReFashion Lab built on the notion of customisable identity, and was intended as an experimental platform to test specific scenarios of interaction between people, space and media. 'Look and show' interactive wearables placed in the boutique's Opinion Room were small mirrored items of jewellery. By holding them up at a full-scale mirror on the wall, visitors triggered the reflections of the faces of others who had been there and left messages.

Top left and right
MetaMirror, designed with Tomato Interactive, London, was an interactive wall that offered many possibilities. While people were trying on clothes it could present an animation, but could also become a customisable mirror with certain distorting effects.

Right
The Delay mirror replayed the viewer's image with a three-second time lag, giving the person a new slant on him- or herself.

fashion and jewellery designers from Germany and Sweden. The project was exhibited in two major galleries in Sweden in 2001.

'We wanted to see what other social interactions could take place in a fashion store, besides buying products, exploring relationships and thresholds in the space.' The Smart Studio team established ubiquitous technology in the space, without involving the visitor in complicated, technical ways of interacting with it. As a result, the modes of interaction could be understood as an augmentation, or extension, of existing real-world experiences. 'We can enjoy the immediate physical nature of our built environments blended with the ephemeral nature of animated digital media, interactive ambient sounds or kinetic events that react to the presence of visitors,' explains Schneidler. 'The space becomes an active interface to information and ambience. Beyond the static notion of architectural design, spatial programme and digital content start to converge as a new entity.'

The MetaMirror was developed with the help of Tomato Interactive in London, who created an interactive wall with an animated display that automatically switched from animation to a personalised mirror with the help of a special radio-frequency chip that tagged the fashion items. Each item was identified individually, given a date and name and recorded by the camera. The mirror was plugged into the Smart Studio's special media infrastructure, linking space, artefact and media into one entity. It worked a bit like the torch in the Avesta project, because it used the information it layered as a metasurface, and in the process changed the ambience of the space. In addition, 'the link between ephemeral media and physical object created new conceptual entities that were hybrid objects,' explains Schneidler. 'They inhabited the real world and virtual space at the same time, challenging cultural notions of value and ownership relating to physical commodities.'

Scanner worked with the team on an ambient interactive radio chip that picked up sound items stored for each fashion item. When the item was brought out onto the shop floor, as a result of antennae hidden behind the scenes that advised the system to play the corresponding sound configuration at a particular location, its presence contributed a new, yet synchronised musical composition replayed as a soundscape.

Another ReFashion Lab element was the Delay mirror, not a brand-new concept but a very simple one that replayed the image of the person in front of the mirror

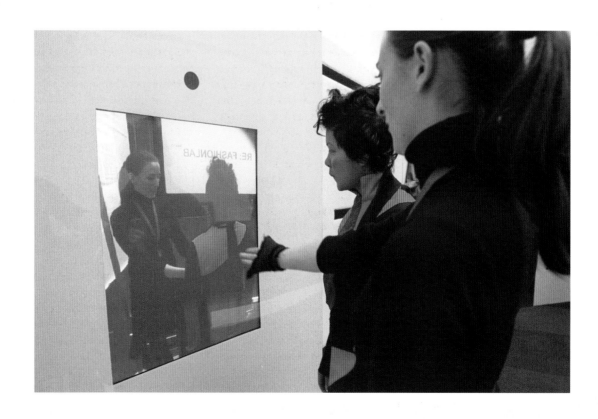

Above
ReFashion Lab, Moderna Museet and Liljewalchs Konsthall, Stockholm, 2001
The Peek, designed by Christiane Posch, gave a revealing and adjustable glimpse through the boutique's shop window. Because it was a projection, it could change its nature, becoming opaque or transparent, tiny or completely opened up.

Notes
1 The Interactive Institute is being built up stage by stage in the form of studios located throughout Sweden. Each one has a unique orientation and director. The core members of its Smart Studio are Ingvar Sjöberg, Thomas Broomé, Sarah Ilstedt, Arijana Kajfes, Fredrik Petersson, Tobi Schneidler and Pablo Miranda.
2 www.smart.tii.smart/projects.
3 www.refashionlab.com.

delayed by three seconds, triggering an immediate provocation in self-perception. 'We had fantasies about it being useful, but the actual effect was more dramatic. Children used it like a playground. Grown-ups were more self-conscious.'

The Peek, designed by Posch, was a projected floating peephole in the shop window that changed its projection, ranging from opaque and of keyhole proportions to much larger and transparent as the visitor approached, creating an unusual visual gateway into the shop. 'Look and show' interactive wearables like jewellery worked in conjunction with the Opinion Room, a play on a conventional changing room, which allowed visitors to leave their comments. It contained a full-scale mirror, and when the visitor held a tiny wearable piece of mirrored jewellery up to the wall, the reflections of the faces and forms of others who had been there before and left messages appeared, visiting him or her from data space.

'A great deal of technical projects exist,' says Schneidler, 'that are mainly engineering driven and miss out on important cultural effects, sensibilities and experiences. Functionality and usability are important ingredients of interactive design, but cultural scenarios and an engaging design language are probably equally important to the understanding, acceptance and enjoyment of new types of interfaces.'

All of the installations in the ReFashion Lab demonstrated, through example, how real physical space and interactive technologies can converge into a new model for architectural experiences. The dynamic interlacing of the potentials of media and communication within the design of the built environment is the key to understanding the field beyond its aesthetic potential, Schneidler explains. Architecture can now become truly dynamic and adaptive. 'The bandwidth of possible solutions is so big, making it hard to pin things down.' And architects, he feels, are often trying to be much too dogmatic about their position: 'It took me a while to get rid of that.' However, he doesn't feel that there are so many variables in new architectural programmes, nor so many new qualities possible purely on a sculptural and spatial level. The developments he describes, along with their implied new logic of building, appeal to him not so much because of their aestheticism, but because they offer scope to propel new social scenarios.

'Architects could learn to think about design as something happening on a ranging scale of immediacy, as an architect always tries to look at things from the top down,' he adds. But at the same time, Schneidler is anxious not to do down architectural sensibilities, but to stress what makes them of continued value – he feels that strategically, interaction designers can learn a lot from architects, 'who are trained to look at entities and map connections between contexts'. ⌂

Jason Bruges:

Light and Space Explorer

Designing bespoke pieces for a range of public and commercial projects, interactive architect Jason Bruges redefines the role of the architect as maker of responsive environments, an identity closer to that of the artist. Lucy Bullivant explains how his application of state-of-the-art technologies enables Bruges to push the boundaries both in terms of his exploration of light, sound and space and the materials he uses.

Jason Bruges is one a few practitioners in the UK making a full-time living from interactive architecture. His work combines environmental awareness and advanced technical skills, and is diverse in range, including interactive light sculpture, interactive environments and installations. Bruges set up in business on his own three years ago and now works with a small team of people designing interactive projects internationally, for clients ranging from BT, Ericsson, T-Mobile, Alsop Architects, Camden Council, BT Openworld, Nutopia, The Hospital Group, the Victoria Miro Gallery and the Venice Biennale.

Recently he designed an interactive light curtain for The Hospital, the music, film and art space initiated by musician Dave Stewart. Last year he was nominated for an interactive BAFTA (British Academy of Film and Television Arts) award for Auroral Synapse, a collaboration with Anna Hill and Martyn Ware, installed

at the Kilkenny Arts Festival in Ireland, and he is developing an interactive exhibition space for Amnesty International.

In June 2004, for UK Architecture Week, visitors to the Victoria & Albert Museum had a rare opportunity to experience Bruges' Infinity Ceiling, an 'interactive skyscrape' with proportions reminiscent of a Baroque Quadri Riportati arrangement. Clouds on the lightweight ceiling floated above the heads of passers-by. At first this was seemingly random. Then, the wind seemed to shift direction, with increasing dependence on the motion of the viewer. As

Opening page
Sky chandelier, Gloucestershire Royal Hospital, Gloucester, due for completion 2005
A shimmering array of cast-acrylic teardrops suspended over the 10-metre-high glazed courtyard of the outpatients wing of this major NHS Trust hospital, a room with restricted views of the sky, traces the patterns and textures of sky movement. A catenary structure designed with structural engineers Adams Kara Taylor, it incorporates a camera/sensor.

Above
Phosphor Field, Poole, Dorset, due for completion 2005
An outdoor installation for Poole Borough Council on roundabout sites at the road gateways to Poole. When the wind blows it triggers a 'floating field of phosphorescent light', a cluster of lightweight masts with LED lights and wind-sensing fibre woven across their mandrels. Depending on how strong the wind is, a range of animated light sequences can be experienced by car drivers and passers-by.

Right
Litmus, Rainham Marshes, Essex, 2004–05
The experience of driving through the marshy, postindustrial terrain crossed by the A13 and now undergoing redevelopment is enlivened by four installations commissioned by Havering Borough Council on roundabouts. Each is a stalk-like structure of steel and transparent acrylic panels with, at its top, clusters of coloured LED lights, individually colour coded, that respond to environmental data.

more people stopped to look up, the clouds built up on the horizon and the process began again.

Trained as an architect at Oxford Brookes University and the Bartlett School of Architecture, UCL, Bruges worked with Foster & Partners for three years before moving to Imagination to become a senior designer and interactive design consultant. His work pushes the boundaries of technical possibilities, whilst focusing on a piece's interaction with its environment and the individual. 'My compositions are not complete without the interaction of an individual. Each person experiencing one of my works will have their own unique memory of it,' he says.

The installations are site specific, interactive bespoke designs utilising state-of-the-art technologies and materials. 'I push the boundaries of the materials I use,' says Bruges. One theme they have in common is that they explore the dynamic and ephemeral qualities of light and interactivity. Most use self-illuminating light technology or light projection, which responds dynamically through sensors to a range of stimuli. Projects develop out of a process of rigorous research and development, and a creative response to the environment.

For the NHS Trust in charge of the new Gloucestershire Royal Hospital, Bruges is working on a sky chandelier to enhance the large glass-sided courtyard in the outpatients wing, which has few direct views of the sky. Consultation with the staff helped to generate the design and change its course from an initial camera obscura concept reflecting views of the landscape, to one that was contrast-based, due to the fact that the outpatients for this particular wing, some of them waiting for up to two hours, were mostly partially sighted. A catenary structure designed with Adams Kara Taylor, its formal cloud-like nature maps and tracks the movement of the sky – its patterns, textures and cloud formation. A feature being developed with the Meteorological Office will allow viewers to perceive particle sizes of individual clouds, so on overcast days people will still be able to see the patterns.

The 10 x 7.5 metre courtyard is split into a 3 x 3 metre grid with the footprint of the installation occupying the middle part, itself split into a further grid.

The digital feed from the camera/sensor is broken up into pixels, and then mapped onto a location in the structure, which has cast-acrylic teardrops, the sparkle and luminosity of which change in real time. After the first visualisations were shown to the client, and an exhibition of his designs displayed at the hospital, Bruges confessed: 'I've been amazed at how people have understood the piece.' This was likely to be to do with the clarity of the design allied with the fact that 'the custom of looking at the sky is an old one, quite prehistoric across all cultures.'

On roundabout sites marking the gateways to Poole, in Dorset, Bruges has installed Phosphor Field for Poole Borough Council. A cluster of slender, lightweight masts sits on the isolated islands. Frictionless wind-sensing, side-emitting fibre has been woven around the mast mandrels during their fabrication. Once erected, the wind blowing across the sites generates a floating field of dancing phosphorescent light, and the masts flex in response, causing the LEDs to illuminate a 'light cloud' above the roadway. 'It is a visual metaphor for the Beaufort scale of wind, with different animated sequences being triggered by varying wind conditions on the sites,' says Bruges.

Another environmental project is Litmus, a number of interactive installations on roundabouts along the A13 road at Rainham Marshes, Essex, a postindustrial landscape and transitory place between built-up area and marshland that is slowly being redeveloped, commissioned by Havering Borough Council. Installed in October 2004, they look like stalks and are made of transparent acrylic panels with a steel substructure with clusters of coloured LED lights above. For each site they are colour coded, acting as orientation devices, a byproduct of the piece. They respond to their environmental data and display this to the drivers of passing traffic. The installation can be viewed remotely on an online microsite and the parameters of the data source change to affect the sensors'

algorithm technology. 'The roundabouts act like giant litmus papers that sense and respond to the immediate local environment,' says Bruges. Visually, they are quite abstract, a bit like the variable message displays (VMDs) on motorways, but draw attention to how the surrounding landscape is being regenerated.

Memory Wall, a mnemonic light matrix in the eighth-floor lobby of the new Puerta America Hotel in Madrid, which has been designed by various architects, responds to movement through the lobby space. The motions of the individuals inside act as a catalyst for an ambient visual projection, in which motion and form are captured, filtered and projected onto the wall surfaces in a continuous loop, with memories of the day building up on them. For this installation, Bruges worked with Kathryn Findlay, who was the architect of the eighth floor of the hotel building. Her architecture has organically shaped the walls with off-white surfaces, onto which Bruges' faceted LED matrix curtain of glass-reinforced gypsum is laid flush with the surface as if it is pigmented, storing layers of activity and memories. Through a series of hidden cameras that act as sensors and capture activity in the lobby, the matrixes of light act as interpretations of the live camera feed.

'The way the walls mimic activity in the lobby is bio-mimetic,' says Bruges. Because the matrix is made of fibre-optics and because the light activity is layered, colours leak out and 'bleed' into the wall – the sensors read in such a way that a whole spectrum or textural gamut of colour appears throughout the space, the first time such an effect has been realised. The light activity also copies the spectrum colours in the lobby, a 'bit like pointillism – the piece is a bit like a palimpsest in the wall'.

'With a lot of the pieces, I talk about the reactions of the lights as being choreographed, because you can predetermine the light response,' says Bruges. It is the human reaction that is uncharted. With all his work, 'there is almost a complexity in trying to keep it simple. There's a bit of a magical element, but I'm not trying to do hundreds of effects or layers of ideas. There's usually one rationale behind a piece.' As for the technology, it is 'getting more complex, but at the same time simpler to use'. ∆

Above
Memory Wall, Puerta America Hotel, Madrid, 2004
The new Puerta America Hotel in Madrid, featuring rooms designed by notable architects including Zaha Hadid, Ron Arad and Kathryn Findlay, features an eighth-floor lobby interactive installation that Bruges calls a mnemonic light matrix. It filters movement and form, which are projected on the wall surfaces in a continuous loop of built-up memories of the day, thanks to a faceted LED matrix curtain of glass-reinforced gypsum containing hidden cameras. The layered fibre-optics emit a textured array of different tones around the lobby.

BIX Matrix
realities:united
Kunsthaus Graz
Austria

Top
Looking a little like the body of an animal, the biomorphic structure of the new Kunsthaus in Graz floats above a glass foyer. More than 1,200 individually shaped, opaque, acrylic glass panels wrap the whole volume of the building like a skin. realities:united created BIX matrix, an integrated media technology skin for the building, which displays a constantly changing texture of images and displays designed by artists and curators.

Bottom
The Kunsthaus' media facade faces the river and the city centre, a part-transparent, part-opaque electronic membrane across the building's eastern facade. On the roof is a viewing gallery, and to the left an original iron-framed structure converted into exhibition space.

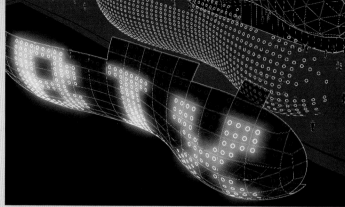

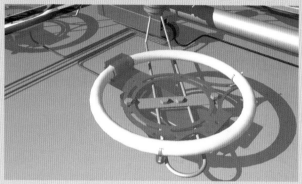

Electronic surfaces to buildings that carry sounds and imagery are not new in a world of high-technology billboards. However, BIX Matrix, writes **Lucy Bullivant**, is integral to the architecture of the Kunsthaus in Graz – an innovative and low-tech skin with its own software for artists and curators to use.

Top left
The BIX matrix electronic skin is made up of 930 light rings covering an area 20 metres high and 40 metres wide, on which low-resolution images, films and animations are presented. On the ground floor is a glazed café area facing the river.

Top right
Exploded visualisation of the BIX matrix showing the integration of architecture, technology and message.

Middle right
Detail of one of the 930 fluorescent light rings, a conventional fluorescent lamp of 40 watts with a diameter of 40 centimetres. Its brightness can be adjusted at an infinite variability of 20 frames per second, so that each lamp acts as a pixel. The rings form their own layer beneath the building's acrylic glass panel surface.

Bottom right
Implementation planning of the BIX matrix.

Autumn 2003 heralded the birth of a new building, biomorphic in structure with a symbiotic interactive architectural element. The opening of the eagerly awaited Kunsthaus in Graz, Austria, designed by architects Peter Cook (co-founder of Archigram and, until 2004, chairman of the Bartlett School of Architecture, UCL) and Colin Fournier, professor of architecture and urbanism at the Bartlett, synthesises an innovative language of form with the historical ambience of the western side of this exceptionally well-preserved city. Graz Altstad (the old part of the town) was a previously disadvantaged district recently designated a UNESCO World Heritage Centre. Bringing a major permanent contemporary cultural focus to the area, the compact Kunsthaus radically redefines its public spaces.

But apart from this, while the new Kunsthaus is conceived aesthetically as a 'black box of

hidden tricks', its outer skin, which faces the river and the city centre with the Schlossberg (castle hill) in the background, is a part-transparent, part-opaque electronic membrane never previously realised in this form. Under the building's acrylic facade on the river side is an intermediate electronic membrane on top of a mesh layer forming the internal covering. Designed by the Berlin-based architects realities:united[1] led by Jan and Tim Edler, it is a unique, effective and imaginative use of technology, a 900-square-metre media skin called BIX[2] (big pixels) integrating architecture, technology and visual message, used as an instrument and platform for artistic production in a new level of mediation.

'In our designs we synchronise architecture, information technology and communication content to develop design concepts, technologies and action strategies that unite the material "old" reality with the immaterial "new" realities, which increasingly overlay and augment the present,' say realities:united. 'Audiovisual media, global communications and information networks and computer interfaces constitute a synthetic fabric that coats the appearance of the everyday world ... we must begin to develop truly integrative patterns for design, semantic exchange and actual utilisation.'

BIX is actually quite a low-tech method using 930 circular fluorescent 40-watt light-ring tubes integrated

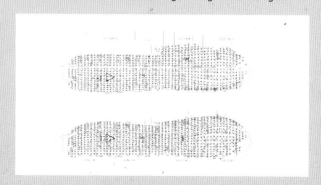

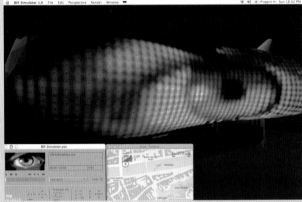

into each section of the facade, mounted in between the acrylic and the membrane. As a result, the resolution of the matrix is very low, with only 930 pixels – 0.2 per cent of the pixels in a conventional TV screen – that are black and white. However, the solution allows the design to be fully integrated into the architecture. Using conventional big-screen display technology, and assuming the same budget, the surface area would have needed to have been a hundred times smaller.

Each ring of light functions as a pixel centrally controlled by computer. The brightness of the lamps can be individually adjusted at an infinite variability with 20 frames/second, which allows images, films, animations and text to be displayed, transforming the Kunsthaus's skin into a giant low-resolution computer display[3] visible from a considerable distance within the city.

At night the form disappears, leaving the dancing light patterns to work their magic. Together they turn the blue bubble into a low-resolution screen that can display simple image sequences and varying text streams. Up close, they become totally abstract. realities:united sees the relative coarseness and monochromacity of the visuals as an advantageous limitation, for new technology of large screens ages extremely fast, and this solution saves constant upgrading and costs.

Software tools evolved as part of the project. BIX Director allows the user to compose a program to be shown on the facade, and BIX Simulator enables artists to look at the results of their productions on a real-time 3-D computer simulation. The tools were a key aspect of the project because they make the production of artistic content possible, at a large scale and for public laboratory experiments. Understandably, the architects hoped the Kunsthaus curators would not use it for advertising; they prefer the idea of a media

facility as an urban playground for the public, but run by architects. 'Architects need to develop a culture of the changing facade,' say the Edlers.

The Kunsthaus is planned as a multidisciplinary venue for exhibitions, events and other means of presenting art, new media and photography. A glass-walled ground floor with a bar, function rooms and amenities leading off the Kunsthaus foyer heralds the start of the moving ramp travelator to the upper exhibition spaces and studio for electronic art. Like a bubble of air, the bluish acrylic skin of the Kunsthaus floats above its glass-walled ground floor. Spanning up to 60 metres in width, the biomorphic construction envelops two large exhibition spaces without additional supports. The skin is made of 1,200 panels of 2-centimetre translucent blue Plexiglass, a pliable acrylic plastic sheet, held in place on a triangulated steel-grid structure by a custom-designed clamp system made using computer-aided manufacture. As a symbiotic part of this structure, BIX enables the institution to present a transparency of information and content, and to further 'develop methods for dynamic communication between building and surroundings, between content and outside perception', explain the architects.

Peter Pakesch, artistic director of the Kunsthaus, inaugurated the building's intelligent 'skin' promisingly with Eintönen (tuning in), a series of sound installations synchronised with the lighting program (for instance, by Max Neuhaus), to set the mood for the opening

exhibition 'Einbildung'. The artistic roll call for the exhibition included Angela Bulloch, Jan Dibbets, Olafur Eliasson and Bridget Riley, and it took perception as its theme, in the sense of the creative science of the processes within our brains that create images and ideas. realities:united approved of these initial efforts. The company is well aware that the relationship between architecture and its facade has long been a topic for debate, and believes that 'architecture is not an episodic instrument but a performative act that happens all the time'.

Their collaboration has brought a modus operandi for the architecture that enables it to transmit and radiate artistic activities within the city that 'you read like a clock tower'. The light matrix is an amorphous zone tailored to the complex shape of the building, fading away at the edges, giving the impression that the biomorphic shape creates the light patterns from within itself. realities:united describes the installation as 'an architectural enabler', and emails to the company from all over the world testify to its popularity. BIX's credibility as a venture was such that it won over the judges of the German Art Directors Club, an advertising rather than architectural professional body, who selected it for a 'Golden Nail' award in 2004, the first time a project in the 'communication in space/cultural projects' had been given such an award.

There have been a few complaints that the program shown on the facade, which was evolved by the Kunsthaus curators, is not changed often enough. realities:united's deep research into BIX's potentials meant they had confidence in proposing to take on this curatorial role, but the content has been managed in-house since the opening. BIX is a new medium in terms of resolution, scale, format and urban setting, and it is clear that it will take a while before curators and artists learn how to fully exploit its potentials.

The architecture of the Kunsthaus represents – at a point in architectural history when there is maximum design freedom – an intentional experiment rather than a formula. It is iconic, but furthermore intends to be a statement typifying a more open form of European architecture – and artistic mediation. As Cook explains, 'We are episodic, not polemical.' His and Fournier's architecture is 'quite theatrical, with a sequence of events and revelations. It shouldn't be seen as static.' The pair always envisaged their facade as a chameleonic, interactive skin, bringing the art inside to the urban surface, just as Rogers and Piano anticipated a high degree of flexibility in the image of the Pompidou Centre in Paris. What they have in common is a design solution that allows for the life of the building to contribute to its meaning, rather than being an overarching aesthetic formula visitors take in passively.

The Kunsthaus' fusion of architecture and design software, and media technology, defines a new standard in architecture – an approach that is likely to be a guiding strength of many future urban building schemes. △

Above
An audiovisual artwork plays on the facade of the Kunsthaus, transforming it into a low-resolution screen displaying simple image sequences. It can also carry varying text streams.

Notes
1 www.realities-united.com.
2 www.bix.at.
3 A 10-minute video documentary about BIX can be viewed at rtsp://media.heimat.de/r/e/rea lu_bix_fulldocu_352ns.rm.

Ada:
the Intelligent Room

A multidisciplinary team based at the Institute of Neuroinformatics, ETH, Zurich, was responsible for Ada: the intelligent room, an interactive space conceived of as a human being that responded to visitors at Expo 02, the Swiss national exhibition at Neuchâtel, where it was launched, writes Lucy Bullivant.

Imagine a creature that lives, behaves, communicates and feels – and imagine that it is a room called Ada. Ada, the intelligent room, which is far away from any known creature, is a multimodal immersive interactive space developed for Expo 02, the Swiss national exhibition held at Neuchâtel, Switzerland. She was conceived by a multidisciplinary team of 25 people led by psychologist Paul Verschure,[1] working at the Institute of Neuroinformatics,[2] University ETH Zurich in Switzerland.

As an artificial organism, Ada has the ability to interact and communicate with her visitors, but that is because she is a project based on the latest research in neuroinformatics. As project leader Verschure explains, the intention was to trigger a public debate about the application and implication of brain-based technology on our future society. In the context of the growing

number of dynamically modifiable components within large multipurpose buildings, Ada, with her high level of behavioural integration and time-varying and adaptive functionality, is a rare exercise in the creation of living architecture.

Named after Lady Ada Lovelace, one of the pioneers of computer science, Ada functioned continuously for 10 hours a day over six months, far longer than the average technical infrastructure found in most art exhibitions. But then the project totally depended upon her real-time interactions. She is a functional creature, programmed to balance visitor density and flow, identify, track, guide and group specific visitors, and play games with them. The experience is well sequenced: visitors approach a waiting area – a 'conditioning tunnel' – where they can witness a staged introduction to Ada's components and their functions. They then enter a 175 square metre space, an octagonal room where all interaction with Ada occurs.

Ada locates and identifies them by using her senses of vision, audition and touch. A 360-degree ring of 12 LCD video projectors has given her advanced visual display capabilities, and these allow her to express her behavioural mode and internal emotional states to visitors.

In a corridor around this space – the 'voyeur space' – visitors can observe the activities without interacting directly. Next they enter the Brainarium, a technical display room that shows the internal processing states of Ada, which has windows providing views into the interaction space. On the way out, visitors can pass through the Explanatorium, a room explaining and discussing the key technologies behind Ada and, if they want to see backstage, the Lab area, the operating room containing more than 30 custom-built computers.

Once visitors are inside the central interaction space, Ada locates and identifies them by using her senses of vision, audition and touch. A 360-degree ring of 12 LCD video projectors has given her advanced visual display capabilities, and these allow her to express her behavioural mode and internal emotional states to visitors. Ada does this by using the screens as a single virtual display; she can render 3-D objects in real time, and display live video. For instance, she records images of 'interesting' visitors and then displays them on the visual synthesiser.

Her 'skin' is made up of 360 floor tiles, each of which is made up of pressure sensors, neon tubes and a microcontroller. Using this extensive surface, Ada can track her visitors, test their responsiveness to visual and sensual cues, and interact with them through different types of games. Local visual effects can also be created with the RGB-coloured neon lights in each tile, rather like a chameleon. A ring of ambient lights sets the overall visual emotional tone of the space, while nine gazer lights with pan, tilt and zoom capabilities make up Ada's 'eyes' (although she does not take the form of a representational concept in this

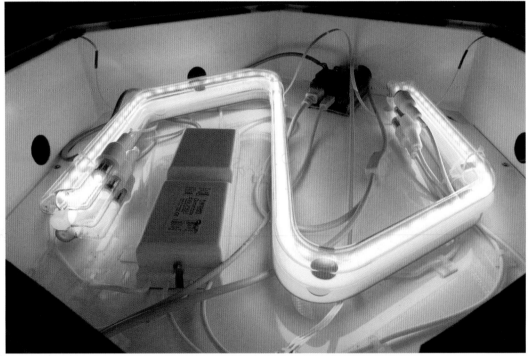

Previous page, top left
Ada's main high-ceilinged space with vibrant illuminated floor tiles undergoing testing before the start of Expo 02. Visitors to the exhibition could stand and move about on the tiles fitted with pressure sensors and change their colours.

Previous page, bottom left
The site of Expo 02 was a platform over the lake of Neuchâtel. Ada was housed in the wooden building under the roof structure on the left. Artificial plastic reeds in the lake bed flashed at night around the perimeter.

Previous page, bottom right
Promotional shoot for Ada in progress, just before the opening of Expo 02.

Top
A training session for the Ada exhibit guides before the start of the exhibition. Ambient light created an atmospheric setting in the space.

Middle
Inside one of Ada's patented floor tiles, showing the red, green and blue neon tubes, the small control board and the internal cabling.

Bottom
Ada tracked single visitors by lighting up the tiles on which they were standing.

Opposite, top
Ada tracked multiple visitors by lighting up floor tiles, and focusing attention on them with her light fingers.

Opposite, bottom
The 'conditioning tunnel' at the main entrance to Ada. Here, visitors were introduced to her individual elements via a sequence of illuminated wall panels.

also able to perform a simple form of baby talk which imitates what she hears from her visitors. Ada also has a number of movable light fingers for pointing at individual visitors or for indicating different locations in the space.

To convince even the most sceptical visitors that Ada shares the properties of a natural organism, the design team made sure the operation of the space was coherent in real time, understandable to most people and offered a sufficiently rich range of possible interactions for visitors to feel the presence of 'a kind of basic unitary intelligence'. The four basic behavioural functions Ada incorporates – tracking, identifying, grouping and playing with visitors – represent a set of interconnected, interdependent, simultaneously evolving internal processes. This stems from the fact that the underlying software is a mixture of simulated neural networks, agent-based systems and conventional

Notes
1 And Kynan Eng, Andreas Bäbler, Ulysses Bernardet, Mark Blanchard, Marcio Costa, Tobi Delbrück, Rodney J Douglas, Klaus Hepp, David Klein, Jonatas Manzolli, Matti Mintz, Fabian Roth, Ueli Rutishauser, Klaus Wassermann, Adrian M Whatley, Aaron Wittmann and Reto Wyss.
2 Its mission is 'to discover the underlying principles in artificial systems that interact with the real world', quoted in Ada: Buildings as Organisms, Kynan Eng and the other team members, abstract of paper presented at 'Game, Set and Match', 13–14 November 2001, Faculty of Architecture, TU Delft, the Netherlands. This and other papers can be found at www.ini.ethz.ch/~ada.

sense as most robots generally do on some level). Two sets of microphones in the ceiling allow Ada to detect different types of sounds, and where they are generated – a pretty challenging prospect in a noisy and echo-filled space with people constantly milling about, as the design team admits.

Ada's capability in terms of sound effects derives from a synthetic musical composition system called Roboser, that creates a 12-voice behavioural mode controlled soundscape. She is

procedural or object-oriented software. Continuing system upgrades incrementally increased Ada's capabilities throughout the four-month exhibition, so that she interacted with visitors, expressed herself and grew – just like human beings.

The public reaction to the exhibit was overwhelmingly positive, with visitors commenting on their deep and playful experience of Ada. According to the team: 'The different modalities of Ada were balanced so that visitors were drawn into a holistic perspective of artefacts and themselves.' ∆

THE LISTENING POST

Ben Rubin and Mark Hansen

A collaborative visual and sonic artwork drawing on research into Internet chatrooms and forums, the Listening Post harnesses the energy of virtual conversation and converts fragments into an evocative experience. **Lucy Bullivant** discusses with its American creators the making of the Listening Post, which has been exhibited at the Brooklyn Academy of Music, Next Wave Festival (2001), the Whitney Museum of American Art, New York (2002), MIT List Visual Arts Center and La Villette, Paris (2004).

Artist Ben Rubin and statistician Mark Hansen first encountered the work of one another when they took part in the Arts in Multimedia programme staged by the Brooklyn Academy of Music and Lucent Technologies in 1999/2000, which brought together artists and scientists. Rubin is a sound designer and multimedia artist whose installations and performance works have been exhibited internationally. His firm, EAR Studio (www.earstudio.com) established in 1993 and based in Bowery in New York City, provides design, consulting and technical production services to architects, museums, artists, producers and performers, and he has frequently collaborated with Laurie Anderson and Diller + Scofidio,

among others. Hansen works for the Statistics and Data Mining Research Department of Bell Laboratories.

It was after this meeting, involving research into data sonification, that the duo evolved a joint project – Listening Post, an installation that visualises and vocalises fragments from the vast range of conversations being carried on in thousands of Internet chatrooms, bulletin boards and other public forums. The project stems from Rubin's particular interest in translating data into sound. The texts are read by a voice synthesiser and simultaneously displayed across a suspended grid of more than 200 small electronic screens.

Listening Post is a visual and sonic response to the content, magnitude and immediacy of virtual communication. It works its way through a series of six

Above and opposite
The Listening Post on
exhibition at the MIT List Visual
Arts Center, April 2004. The
installation encourages
reflection on the emotional
power, scope and accessibility
of virtual communication.

movements, each a different arrangement of visual, aural and musical elements, each with its own data processing logic.

Hansen explains that they agreed early on that the project would have a strong social component. He suggested online chatting as an ideal data source, and after a couple of weeks observing the dynamics of active online chatroom forums, he knew he was on the right track. Over the next few months, the ideas were refined in public performances, academic talks and publications. 'There were no – well, few – disciplinary divides in the process that produced the space. Ben had as much input in data collection and modelling as I did on questions of design and aesthetics.'

They set about looking for data that 'they could find some emotional energy in'. Rubin was sceptical at first, but became convinced when they began listening to the chat: 'Chat turns out to be data that has stories to tell. It had some unexpected emotional qualities that felt universal and human. Taken together, the messages carry with them the sense of the need to connect with people.' At first they listened to statistical representations of websites, and then to actual language from chatrooms, when 'a kind of music began to emerge – the messages started to form a giant cut-up poem, fragments of discourse juxtaposed to form a strange quilt of communication'.

'Anyone who types a message in a chatroom and hits "send" is calling out for a response. Listening

Post is our response – a series of soundtracks and visual arrangements of text that respond to the scale, the immediacy and the meaning of this torrent of communication.' The audience is invited to watch and listen to the piece, rather than directly intervene. People's reactions have tended to be emotional reactions to the content itself, Rubin explains.

Curator Debra Singer, who is based at the Whitney Museum where the Listening Post was exhibited in 2002, observed that 'while participating in a chatroom is social, it is usually solitary and isolating – just the lone person in front of the keyboard – and so what this installation does is give you a sense of that collective global community, and the diversity and scale of Internet conversations and exchange'.

The Listening Post receives chat data in real time. 'Every word that enters our system was typed only seconds before by someone, somewhere. The irregular staccato of these arriving messages form the visual and audible rhythms of the work,' Rubin adds. He goes on: 'The sound-generating systems are constructed almost as wind chimes, where the wind is in this case not meteorological but human, and the particles that move are not air molecules but words. At some level, Listening Post is about harnessing the human energy that is carried by all these words, and channelling that energy through all the mechanisms of the piece.' ꭰ

Tate in Space
ETALAB

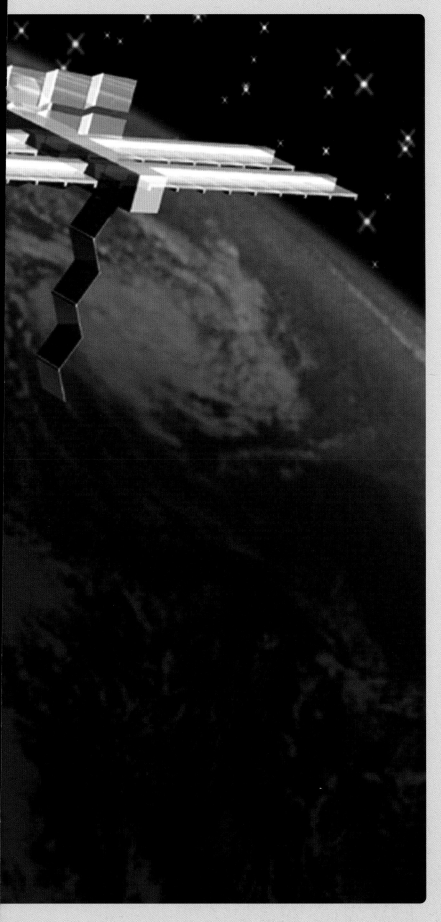

For four minutes of zero gravity, Virgin will soon be offering galactic travel 60 miles out into space in three years time, at a price of £115,000. Eventually, package holidays will follow. With the Hilton allegedly having bought a piece of the moon, commerce has really begun to buy into outer space. Tate in Space, a speculative gallery existing in microgravity, takes this reality firmly in hand, writes **Lucy Bullivant**, with the idea of a Tate gallery satellite. It was designed by ETALAB, run by architects Danielle Tinero and Opher Elia-Shaul, one of three architectural practices commissioned by artist Susan Collins on behalf of Tate, the UK's premier art institution (the others were Softroom and Sarah Wigglesworth Architects).

The gallery ETALAB (Extra-Terrestrial Architectural Laboratory) proposed responds to the extreme environment of outer space and the unpredictable needs of artists, curators and visitors. It exists in microgravity with the possibility of introducing artificial gravity by varying the speed of rotation about a central axis. The envelope would be made from a smart material based on biomechanics, possessing reactive characteristics similar to those of muscles and the nervous system, which would give artists and curators the power to modify the form, space and levels of gravity across the gallery. Visitors would be able to move freely in all directions without the restrictions of staircases or lifts. A café would float around the gallery in a flexible bubble, and windows, seamlessly integrated into the skin, would expand and contract like the lens of an eye. The gallery – envisaged as a 4.5 x 9 metre module similar to NASA's *Transhab*, would dock at the International Space Station or make solo voyages across the solar system, transforming into a solar sail for sustainable propulsion.

'We envisage Tate in Space as both a real and virtual experience,' says ETALAB's Danielle Tinero. As the ultimate synthesis of artistic and scientific behaviour,

it 'would dock at the existing International Space Station and travel to the moon, or follow its own path through the solar system'. Tinero and Opher Elia-Shaul admit that experiential aspects of the voyage – being in a gallery in outer space, with the movements of people becoming omnidirectional and fluid – would challenge the role of art in such a context. 'This would create the potential for a dynamic new physical and temporal relationship where people, artworks and architecture could interact in zones of zero and partial gravity.' Whatever resulted, however, could be relayed live to earth via webcam. The sealed and pressurised, responsive 30-centimetre-thick envelope (a composite of Nextel, a visco-elastic cellular material, woven Kevlar and Kapton sheets) would maintain a comfortable internal environment, shielding visitors from the extreme range of temperatures in outer space and recycling air and water.

ETALAB designed an interactive interface for experiencing the changing form of their proposal. It features a three-dimensional model that can be accessed online and modified in real time via the Tate in Space website (www.tate.org.uk/space/).

'It's been designed as a prototype for an interface that would enable Tate's artists and curators to define, visualise and work within numerous new configurations of form and gravity, be they fixed or changing, random or prescribed,' says Tinero. 'These characteristics would also be applied to the physical structure of the space gallery, and in due course the interface could be further developed with additional programming.' In due course, the curatorial tool could form the basis of a personalised interface for all Web users, allowing visitors to an online or virtual Tate in Space to shape the spaces, adjust gravity levels and develop virtual exhibitions according to their preferences. 'These preferences could be stored as data files enabling visitors to switch between different versions of their own "personal Tate",' adds Tinero.

'It is intended as an *agent provocateur*,' says Collins, 'a catalyst, structure and space for people to occupy that also invites debate and reflection on the nature of art in space, cultural ambition, and an examining of the role of the institution and the individuals within.' And she also feels that it 'can be viewed as an example of interactive or immersive fiction, with each browser/participant bringing their own extraterrestrial cultural fantasies to the project'. △

Induction House
aether architecture/
Adam Somlai-Fischer

An interactive prototype that treats digital media as physical matter, Induction House proposes a more mutually informing relationship between design and technology, writes Lucy Bullivant.

Induction House V2, 'pixelACHE', Kiasma Museum of Contemporary Art, Helsinki, 2004
A prototype within a series of installations and models investigating how digital media might be treated as physical matter, this created an atmospheric blend of art and architecture. The surface of a computer projection was unfolded onto a translucent structure, creating layers of digital information and the prospect of a nonscreen-based computer environment.

Top
Testing the projection for
the installation of Induction
House in Stockholm, 2004.

Middle
Setting up Induction House
at the 'pixelACHE' exhibition,
Kiasma, Helsinki, 2004.

Bottom
A possible future version
of Induction House.

Note
1 *Vampyrotheuthis Infernalis*,
Immatrix Publications
(Goettingen, Germany), 1987,
p 59.

The Czech philosopher Vilém Flusser, one of the most important media theorists of recent years, who died in 1991, believed that 'what we perceive as reality is a tiny detail from the field of possibilities surging around us, which our nervous system has realized through computation. If all reality is a computation from possibilities, then "reality" is a "threshold" value.'[1] Adam Somlai-Fischer, a young Hungarian architect who runs aether architecture (www.aether.hu), and a teacher at the Architecture and Urban Research Laboratory KTH Stockholm, wants architects to look more closely at the implications of this. In particular, the fact that electronic media saturate our cultural environment, influencing our perceived reality. In fact, he says it is unavoidable: 'Think about how many things you have seen for real, and how many on images and film.'

Somlai-Fischer decided to start from scratch, and 'test new possibilities for real, asking what new architecture could arise from our rapidly developing environment. For this reason, I have decided not to draw plans and sections, as in a regular architectural project using representational methods, but to build prototypes, in a 1:1 scale, that are testing the possibilities of blurring the electronic media into the physical space.'

Induction House is the most advanced prototype Somlai-Fischer, who is also a guest researcher at the Smart Studio of the Interactive Institute in the city working on collaborative projects (see pages 72–8), has designed to date. A set of installations and architectural prototypes, it is aimed at developing a discourse about the design of interactive space and, more precisely, investigating ways of treating digital media as physical matter. The surface of a computer projection is unfolded onto a translucent structure, with the result that 'layers of digital information, behaviour and ambience share projection territories' and create the prospect of a 'nonscreen-based computer environment'.

At its inaugural unveiling at the Kunsthalle in Budapest in October 2003, Induction House was a 100 x 100 x 60 centimetre structure of steel and textiles, based on an algorithm that is a sliced flat plane folded, creating a 100 per cent projectable continuous surface. An electromagnetic-field sensor senses mobile-phone usage, and a set of light sensors the shadows of hands. 'The mobile-phone calls change the electronic weather or projected colour temperature, a process not unlike Usman Haque's Sky Ear project (see pages 8–11). Somlai-Fischer has used exhibitions as a test-bed for evaluating 'how certain issues and spatialities are responded to'.

By the time it was shown in its second version (V2) at 'pixelACHE' at the Kiasma Museum of Contemporary Art in Helsinki, in April 2004, the structure was much larger, at 600 x 300 x 170 centimetres, with 300 physical pixels in a matrix that moved along the projectors' light, creating a 100 per cent projectable volumetric structure. Ultrasonic sensors measured visitors' presence and distance. These first two incarnations used Flash as a projection engine, and to interface this program to sensors, a microcontroller clicking Morse signals on a USB computer mouse. The team initially used these low-tech solutions out of necessity, and then as a choice: 'Through constant reappropriation of existing technologies we create new interfaces that hold connotations towards their original use, so stay familiar, but misplaced in a new context.'

More recently, in the autumn of 2004, Induction House V3 was an 800 x 400 x 200 centimetre carbon-fibre, steel and plastic structure with 400 pixel folds, its spatial flows changed by approaching visitors.

Somlai-Fischer sees that by dissolving the physical structure in 'the flux of interactive media, with media simultaneously becoming actual and spatial', the interaction created is 'symbolic, not really trying to function or process information, but to transform the physical entity in a nonphysical way'. His model for the project is borrowed from the systems thinking of complexity science, with several modes of concepts produced, each informing the other back and forth, developing as a whole system without a predetermined hierarchy. Somlai-Fischer wants to talk about a new relationship between technology and design, in which 'the role and effect of technology reveals a more profound relation between design and design tools', and in the process, as Flusser defined it, it becomes possible to 'turn the automatic apparatus against automation'. ∆

Design City
Tokyo

Below
The renovation by Dennis Wedlick Architect for the Department of Environmental Studies at Vassar College, in Poughkeepsie, New York, supplied eco-friendly interiors in a recycled 19th-century academic building.

Eco Imperative

Below
To divide the space without blocking daylight, the architect mounted silk-screened glass into frames of eco-conscious Richlite, a wood-chip composite derived from managed forests. Text on the glass supplies a potted history of environmentalism.

Below
The sleek resource island, which breaks with the 19th-century feeling of the architecture, showcases key research materials behind glass. Panels of wheat-chaff board display the black-and-white photography printed with an organic dye.

Touring Dennis Wedlick Architect's vest-pocket scheme built for New York's Vassar College, **Craig Kellogg** learns what 'green' means.

Some say it isn't easy being green. A splurge on eco-friendly materials and green methods frequently does add both cost and bother to a renovation. But the Department of Environmental Studies at Vassar College had precious little choice. The department serves to unite students and faculty from various areas of study, with the aim of healing the earth. So sensitively redesigned space for the department would serve as no less than a beacon – a 'billboard', as renovation architect Dennis Wedlick now calls it. For Wedlick, the commission was a rare chance to take ideas about sustainability as far as he could, spurred on by eager clients. 'Their aspirations were perfect and their priorities were perfect,' he says.

Basically, Vassar wanted to minimise toxics and waste. Wedlick's job was to balance 'being image driven' against 'being trendy', so that 'people would not quickly tire of the design, tear it down and throw it away'. To enhance the sense of permanence, the architect and his clients decided that the architecture should preserve the building and 'speak to its history'. The structure was built on the Vassar campus in Poughkeepsie, New York, in the late 19th century, with unnecessarily tall ceilings, large windows and stout wood trim. It's the kind of solid old-fashioned architecture rarely built today and altogether too good to waste.

Demolition for the project included breaching a thick masonry wall. Here, Wedlick installed a large basket-handle arch through the bricks, in a nod to traditional methods of masonry architecture. The resulting open space, to be used by faculty and students for meetings and research, shares daylighting from windows in two adjoining glassed-in private offices. For a small degree of privacy, the glass partitions have been silk-screened with quotations and important dates in the environmental movement.

Throughout, Wedlick avoided by-the-book green solutions and eco-scorekeeping systems such as LEED (Leadership in Energy and Environmental Design) green building ratings. 'Trying to fit within a formula really

Below
Reused furnishings for the project include bentwood Thonet chairs at the workstations and, elsewhere, Eero Saarinen's Tulip chairs and table.

limits your opportunities,' he says. 'And if you meet the minimum criteria, you can become complacent.' Instead, he applied a common-sense strategy he calls 'resource first' – 'a backwards approach'. Even before design begins, Wedlick identifies available building trades, consultants, new technologies and local materials. 'I use what makes the most sense for the project and what is also nearby,' he explains, adding that '90 per cent of materials were either recycled or renewable.' The trim is Richlite, which uses wood chips from managed forests. On the vintage chairs (sturdy Thonet designs the department rescued, in an eco-smart gesture), Wedlick employed upholstery fabric made from recycled plastic bottles. The pattern of the text simply reads: 'waste = food'.

Occasionally, green choices can test even the best client's nerves and schedule. 'When you experiment with new materials, you need more time,' Wedlick says. 'You're asking the client to have patience.' A tight time line was among the constraints for contractors at Vassar, as they 'learned how to put new materials together', the architect notes. In order to finish the space during the summer recess, he conceived most of the elements as modular furniture and prefabricated them off site, a process that began even before changes to the old architecture.

'Based on the client's aesthetic aspirations,' says Wedlick, his new 'furniture' was free to be more modern looking. The 'resource island' incorporates chic black-and-white landscape prints by the photographer William Clift. 'Acoustically, we thought it would be very good to put fabric on the ceilings,' Wedlick says. The resulting illuminated ceiling sculpture is covered with fabric of recycled cardboard, hemp and silk stretched on a steel frame. (The seams should dissolve in case of fire, exposing concealed fire sprinklers.)

Even despite his extra efforts, Wedlick stayed within the budget, though some of the most exotic elements were introduced as options and paid for with supplemental fund-raising. The college found the money for a dimming system to measure the amount of daylight in the room and turn down the fluorescents on sunny days (all the while recording the savings that have resulted). 'We feel one of the goals for sustainable design is to raise awareness.' In this case, the system shows 'the net positive impact you're having,' Wedlick notes.

Then again, and quite literally, you could also smell the difference during construction. 'I would go in and say, "Guys, take a whiff",' the architect says. He specified paints formulated without overpowering and unpleasant volatile organic compounds, going so far as to finish the oak floor with a lovely beeswax mixture. An eco-powered ceiling fan (its solar panel is on the roof) promotes circulation in the office. But in any case: the air stayed remarkably clear. 'Normally, the fumes on a construction site are so intense they give you a headache,' Wedlick says. 'But during construction at Vassar, if somebody had bad breath, you could smell it.' ⌑

Below
An image on the skyline. The upward sweep and curved shape of the De Hoftoren
tower, the new home of the Dutch Ministry of Education, Culture and Science,
make a dramatic impact on The Hague's skyline, and also suggest a ship's prow,
an appropriate image for Holland's geographical situation.

Ministry of Education, Culture and Science, The Hague

In the new Ministry of Education, Culture and Science, designed by Kohn Pedersen Fox (KPF), **Jeremy Melvin** finds a tower that offers civil servants more than a well-appointed view of the Dutch seat of power and Amsterdam on a fine day.

Top
Ground-floor plan. Much of the ground level is devoted to a foyer, with space for displaying art, and a café.

Middle
The staff cafeteria, concealed on the mezzanine level, allows employees to observe comings and goings in the public areas, but to remain hidden from view.

Bottom
Floor plan from the first to the 15th level, showing the maximum floorplate. On the 15th floor is the 'coffee corner' in the prow of the lower-rise wing: above it is a suite of large meeting rooms. In the link between the two wings is a 'special projects area', typical of the strategy of allocating space according to task rather than status.

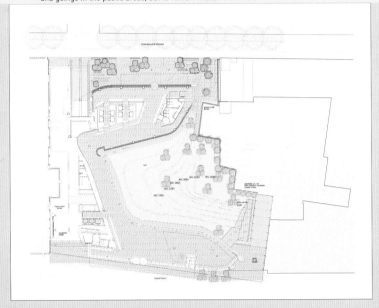

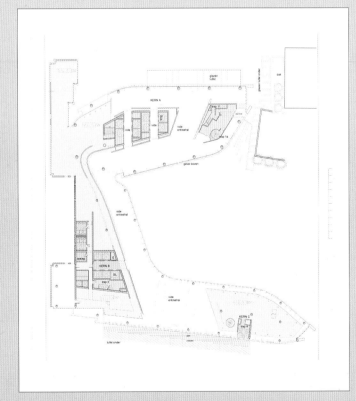

Liberal, tolerant and egalitarian, Holland seems to be an exemplary modern state and evidence that advanced human societies really do have more to offer than their traditional counterparts. But what provoked that human achievement lies at least as much in geological as in historical time, as it stems largely from the need to respond to the country's peculiar geography. Wresting a nation from the sea, the Spaniards and, more recently, protecting it from that lot on the right as you look at the map, has meant every aspect of the state, its organisation and governance has come under detailed scrutiny and has been subjected to rational decision-making. Holland typifies

'the state as a work of art', to borrow the phrase Jacob Burckhardt coined for the republics that emerged with similar characteristics during the Italian Renaissance.[1]

Much of this scrutiny happens in the Ministry of Education, Culture and Science. The Dutch recognise the connection between education and culture, and sensibly separate the latter from sport, which properly belongs in the Ministry of Public Health. In the education ministry the sinews that tie Dutch society together through an excellent universal state-education system and an appreciation of how culture can be undogmatically yet beneficially infiltrated into people's lives, are nurtured, developed and adapted to modern circumstances. Its new home, the 140-metre-tall De Hoftoren tower in The Hague, designed by KPF, is both a 'tool for working in', as Ferdinand van Dam of interior architects Ontwerpgroep Trude Hooykaas puts it, but also a striking urban landmark that addresses some of the aspects of Dutch culture as they are manifested in the city's urban form.

Outwardly it speaks of modernity. Its form seems to sweep upwards in a spiral, making a powerful addition to the skyline. Kevin Flanagan, senior associate partner at KPF and the project's design principal, cites the flowing lines of the great period of Dutch Modernism, and in particular Brinckman and van der Vlugt's van Nelle factory in nearby Rotterdam, as an influence. It also has something of German Expressionism, with its shape, if not materials, recalling Fritz Höger's Chilehaus in Hamburg. The tower itself, as a building type irrespective of its architectural treatment, is one of the few aspects of modern architecture to which Holland made almost no contribution. It is almost inevitably alien. Cesar Pelli and Michael Graves,

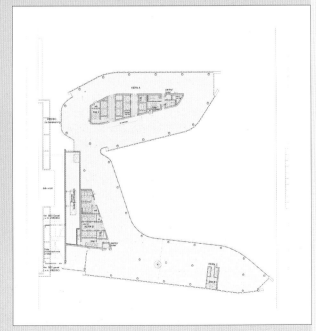

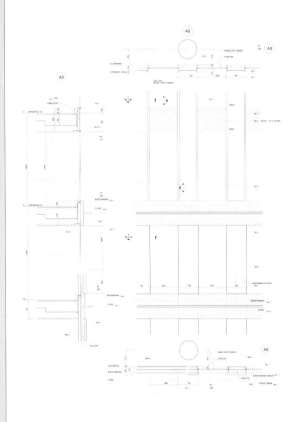

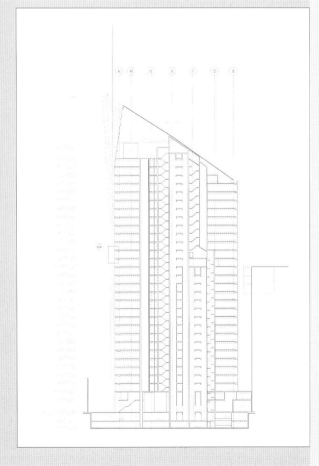

designers of rather lower towers nearby, responded to this condition in typically Postmodern fashion, Graves adding a pair of overgrown Dutch gables and Pelli surmounting his with a clumsy crown. But Flanagan suggests the Dutch share with the Americans a liking for anything new, and the tower is certainly a celebration of height.

But, he continues, the design also grows out of its context, and in Holland the context always consists of encrusted layers of cultural history. The Hague emerged as the Dutch seat of government because parliament moved to be near the monarch, who was reluctant to move from the royal hunting park. The city grew up around a single axis, connecting what is now the Queen's House and the Hofvijver, a late-medieval moated parliamentary complex, and the remains of the hunting forest reach far into the city along that axis, even now stopping only at the Ministry of Finance of Europe's sixth-largest economy. A canal runs at right angles, forming a secondary axis between the city and the dunes at Scheveningen, which keep the North Sea at bay. If one axis reeks of constitutional monarchy, the other evokes Holland's atavistic relationship with water and the forces it contains. Nature and nurture interact, and just off this pregnant junction is the site for De Hoftoren. Its height means ministry employees can see as far as Amsterdam on a clear day, and only need glance down for a spot of revision in Dutch culture. Height becomes part of the didactic programme, a way of appreciating the past that prevents it from overwhelming the present.

Such interwoven symbolism and reference would be unusual in a purpose-designed building: in one which was built as a speculation by the huge finance house ING, it is remarkable, though partly explained by two specific factors. One is that The Hague is purely the seat of government, detached from the capital and financial centre Amsterdam, and Rotterdam which is the other significant economic centre. Ministries and other public bodies are the only tenants likely to take a building of 55,000 square metres and 29 storeys, and the developers know more or less what their needs will be. The other factor is the uncanny skill the Dutch have in devising especially congenial working environments, a condition that developers seem to relish as a challenge rather than an impediment to net-to-gross ratios and profits. In any case, Flanagan says, ING's procurement powers are such that they were able to construct the building for significantly less than it would have cost in London.

Holland in general, and The Hague in particular, show how public and private interests can overlap within a planned economy. The government benefits from offsetting the procurement of such large buildings to private enterprise, but the private sector benefits from the predictability and stability of the market. Such a cosy relationship could easily lead to sclerosis, but this is Holland, where sensible negotiation is preferred to diktat. So while the city council has a responsibility for producing a long-term development plan, it also accepts that the plan will have to change as it unfolds.

De Hoftoren shows this process in action. It lies on the edge of an area master-planned by that guru of po-mo urbanism Rob Krier, which with its Richard Meier city hall and pointy gable towers by Michael Graves seems stuck in the 1980s. Graves did, however, establish a precedent for height, and it was always accepted that whatever was built on the site of De Hoftoren could go higher. KPF turned this to advantage in a design that celebrates height rather than treating it as an embarrassing inflation of a traditional building type, simultaneously gesturing to the public realm at ground level. What could be, security concerns permitting, a public route between the city centre and the main rail terminal that lies alongside De Hoftoren is both monumental and transparent. That this suited the ambitions of the ministry might owe something to coincidence, but it is the sort of coincidence that occurs in a tightly structured society, and the ministry is probably the institution with the single greatest influence over its composition.

KPF's final scheme, which followed a series of abortive proposals for the site, generates its design by interweaving expectations for work-place conditions with the resolution of the relationship between a tower

Top left
The plan form makes a tight urban courtyard, landscaped with wireless workstations.

Bottom left
The large 16th-floor meeting room, where an oval table precludes the hierarchy
of a rectangular layout, a token of the consensus-driven culture of the ministry.

Top right
The mezzanine cafeteria, one of the generous social spaces in the building,
the role of which is to stimulate interaction and communal working.

and its context. The flowing form, reaching 15 floors at one end and rising to 29 for the tower, encloses a small courtyard which is landscaped with wireless workstations, and which conceals an inevitably large cycle-store. Almost the entire ground floor is foyer space, with a café at one end and a gallery at the other. Overlooking the foyer on a concealed mezzanine is a staff cafeteria. This combination of devices suggests a generosity of public space that towers often lack. The adaptable nature of the form means that at low level it can reinforce the block and street pattern, but as it rises it can assume a shape that conceals its bulk from any single viewpoint. It appears to

have a slenderness that only very tall towers, or those with uneconomical floorplates, have otherwise.

Internally these forms bring several benefits. They create numerous expanding, outward-looking forms that are pleasant in themselves, but also readily lend themselves to the ministry's working practices. Driven by consensus, meetings and spaces to hold them in are vital, ranging from small, informal spaces adjacent to regular workstations, to one grand room where 30 people can sit around an oval table and, whether minister or junior civil servant, have equal status and hearing. A typical floor in the tower, for instance, has workstations around the perimeter, grouped into relatively large rooms. Close to the core are 'cabinets', providing small meeting rooms and private study carrels. Throughout, the emphasis is on transparency, with even senior managers sitting in clear glass-walled offices close to lift entrances. Only the minister is genuinely concealed.

De Hoftoren won the 2004 International High Rise Award, and as a concept it goes a long way to showing how towers can make positive contributions to the cityscape, both at the skyline and at ground level. But the design is also remarkable in how, with a relatively small repertoire of large-scale, broad-brush gestures, it manages to relate the needs of a working environment to the symbolic significance of its location and function. ∆

Note
1 'The State as a Work of Art' is the title of the first part of *The Civilisation of the Renaissance in Italy*, Random House (New York), in arrangement with George Allen & Unwin, 1954, first published (in German) in 1860, which sets out, in great detail, Burckhardt's reasons for coining this term.

Top
A clear layout following the shore is articulated on the external corner by a squat, wedge-shaped community centre.

Bottom
There are two basic flat types. The formal language is outspoken and modern.

Lighter Living in the 21st Century:

Fjordparken Himmerland and Marina Fjordparken, Egholm, Denmark

Jane Briginshaw visits a housing scheme in northern Jutland, where the use of timber has tackled concrete's stranglehold over the Danish building industry. A mixed-use scheme, providing social housing and provision for a local cooperative of the marina's sailing-club members, it caters in its internal planning to occupants' needs. Despite being architecturally accomplished, is its cool anonymity devoid of the 'wow' factor that Brits are starting to expect from newbuild?

Think of Denmark and think of northern-lit islands surrounded by water, dissected by fjords and waterways and covered by pine forests. But think again and see the sand, the freely available basic component of concrete and a very profitable industry allowed near-monopoly status in Danish construction since the 1960s.

Aiming to improve construction methods and funding, the Danish government launched a competition to look at different aspects of change. One of the six teams selected, Copenhagen architects Tegnestuen Vandkunsten, has recently completed the largest timber-built project in Denmark and, in the process, has broken the stranglehold of the concrete industry on Danish construction.

A restrained mix of social and cooperative housing looks out over the island of Egholm and Aalborg's cool grey Limfjord. A clear layout following the shore is articulated on the external corner by a squat wedge-shaped community centre. Its strip windows echo the flatness of water and contrast with the sharp verticality of the three-storey flats. Black-painted timber cladding, galvanised-steel balustrades and timber supports fading to grey match the severe beauty of the landscape, giving a defensive face to the fjord edge. Roofs slope away from the fjord, creating a low and open entrance side clad in warm-coloured unpainted timber. The architects are in their element here, responding texturally to the setting, drawing on the skills of landscape-architect partner Svend Algren, growing buildings out of the landscape.

Fjordparken Himmerland, the two northern blocks, consist of 51 units of two, three and four rooms to meet the different needs of this particular group of social-housing tenants. There are also two basic flat types with variations coming from the addition of balconies to the cooperative (southern) housing – Marina Fjordparken – and other minor differences. These might be a door opening directly from the front to create an annexe or a utility room, or a separate rather than en suite bathroom, the access made possible by removing an independent WC. One type has the entrance hall giving access separately to the main bedroom and the living room, the other has all rooms coming off the family room.

The nucleus of the cooperative was formed by the marina's sailing-club members. The varying internal arrangements followed the buyer's individual wishes. The architectural skill lies in finding the maximum number of options within these versions, without being tempted to create a new type. This allows detailing and supervision to be limited, giving greater control over construction quality. It also means that, even though the scheme has to cope with different cost levels and two types of client groups, the overall result remains coherent without an obvious 'rich' and 'poor' side.

The forms of the blocks are outspoken and modern, but elements like the large rough-cut timber-section walkways push Egholm into the rustic idiom that also characterises the architects' work. Inside, the family room is the focus. The workshop-style kitchen at the entrance end allows maximum openness. Every flat has full-height corner windows to view the fjord and the brilliant light. For those with balconies, at this density spaciousness comes before circulation choices, and all the rooms except bathrooms and utility rooms are accessed from the living room. Such deterministic planning intensifies family living. It puts faith in being able to live together, as a family, as a collectivity, and speaks volumes after so many years of practice for Tegnestuen's idealism.

The Danish government wanted to see how the use of timber as the main construction material, with all its sustainable credentials, would work. At the same time it wanted to establish whether construction costs could be reduced, and instructed the architects to collaborate from an early stage with building contractors. The advantages of timber over concrete as a sustainable material are well known: it comes from renewable sources, it takes little energy and causes no pollution in its production, and it is easy and safe to work with and transport. The process was to prove just how difficult it is to bring about change within national markets and fixed building traditions. Although in the UK and other Scandinavian countries timber frames would be used for this sort of construction, here the three-storey frames had to be shipped in from the Baltic, undermining a degree of the project's environmental ambitions.

Concrete's market domination is even enshrined in Denmark's fire regulations which specify its use for structural elements. However, by showing by calculation that timber can provide adequate fire

resistance the architects were able to bring about a change in the regulations. Allowing structural timber to compete with concrete has resulted in a visible reduction in the price of concrete. The architects concluded that the insistence on early collaboration with contractors was not successful, prices tending to increase by reducing competition and shifting the balance too far away from the designer and client.

Tegnestuen Vandkunsten's ecological and social engagement is not limited to the Fjordparken project. In 1998 the practice completed a demonstration project, the Eco House, in Skejby, Aarhus, with two concepts – the Sun House and the Modern Chimney – to establish the extent to which ecology was achievable within a standard public-housing budget. Tegnestuen later collaborated with Copenhagen Energy and a housing association on the first EU-funded photovoltaic (PV) project in Denmark. By retrofitting PV modules to existing housing, and using them both to produce electricity and to preheat ventilation air, it was found that heat savings could pay back the investment within seven years.

This work, completed in 2002, is the latest of many projects by the Copenhagen architects best known for the pioneering rental co-housing community called Tinggarden, built in 1976. Tegnestuen Vankunsten was founded in 1970 by four men of the '68 generation' – Svend Algren, Jens Thomas, Michael Sten Johnsen and Steffan Kragh – who today are still very much in charge of the considerable, mainly housing, output of the practice. Tegnestuen won a national Danish Building Research Institute sponsored competition for low-rise, clustered housing. This project was to be the decisive break with the Modernism that had gone before. It was the first realisation of the idea of a new and alternative housing environment in the form of small, intimate residential enclaves. The idiom was varied and informal and set the tone for residential building in the decades to follow.

In Egholm we are poles apart from the glitzy iconic architecture fashionable in the UK. Here is a project that is accomplished and controlled, one that ably illustrates the practice objective to 'strive for architectural quality in ordinary residential building'. It has been greeted with nothing but enthusiasm by the occupants. It bears out the accepted wisdom that Danish architecture is more influential when it is anonymous than when it is monumental, because of its quality and originality. Given the drama of the setting and all the possibilities that could have unfolded, perhaps this project is just a little too anonymous to UK eyes. ◬

EGHOLM	G 0-29%	F 30-39%	E 40%	D 41-49%	C 50-59%	B 60-69%	A 70-100%
QUALITATIVE							
Space-Interior						B	
Space-Exterior						B	
Location						B	
Community						B	
QUANTITATIVE							
Construction Cost					C		
Cost-rental/purchase					C		
Cost in use					C		
Sustainability						B	
AESTHETICS							
Good Design?						B	
Appeal					C		
Innovative?					C		

This table is based on an analytical method of success in contributing to solution to housing need. The criteria are: Quality of life – does the project maintain or improve good basic standards? Quantative factors – has the budget achieved the best it can? Aesthetics – does the building work visually?

Jane Briginshaw is currently researching and writing, with Bruce Stewart, The Architects' Navigation to New Housing, to be published in autumn 2005 by Wiley-Academy. She is a practising architect and design lecturer at the University of Greenwich, London, and was a local council speaker on housing, and a candidate, for the 2004 European elections.

Below
Big Belt House, Meagher County, Montana, 2000
Cutting patterns for formwork.

Blurring the Lines
Case Study: Digital Housings
An Exploration of Current CAD/CAM Techniques

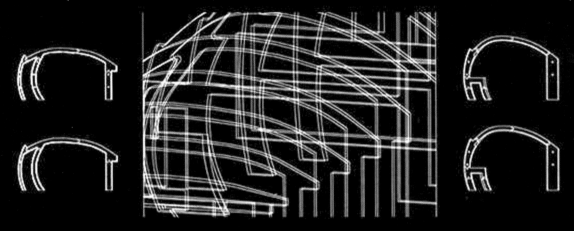

Domestic-scale projects can be a fertile source of technical and design innovations, as shown in a crop of houses designed and built by Massie Architecture. In this fifth instalment of the 'Blurring the Lines' series of CAD/CAM case studies, **André Chaszar** describes some of the novel and effective ways in which digital design and fabrication have entered the realm of single-family housing in the US, and traces the evolution of these techniques in successive applications.

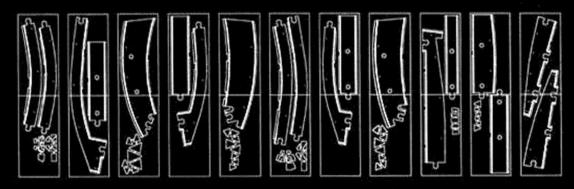

The work of the New-York based firm Massie Architecture, although as yet small in scale, lies at the cutting edge of digital architectural practice in many senses, not the least of which is the firm's extensive and direct experimentation with fabrication and assembly methods that leverage the computer's capabilities to generate and manage complex data, and to carry these data through from the design phase to the construction of a project. Examples drawn from a number of the practice's recent and current projects illustrate the variety of ways in which CAD/CAM can be put to use even on projects of modest scope, thereby attaining the goals of quality and inventiveness (both formal and technical), as well as economy. As the examples show, it is useful for the designers to have a large measure of control over the fabrication equipment and onsite logistics when undertaking such experimental work.

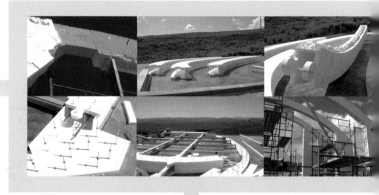

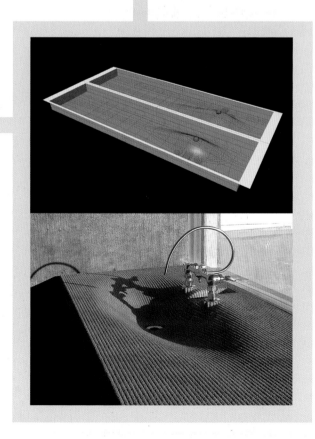

Big Belt House, Meagher County, Montana, 2000

One of Massie Architecture's earliest projects, the Big Belt House, employed digital design and fabrication methods at a variety of scales to achieve a building of gently curving forms harmonising with the landscape, with furnishings and other details enhancing relations between the house and its occupants.

At the scale of the building frame, curved concrete beams were cast in custom-made polystyrene forms. The rigid foam sheets were CNC-cut from the architects' digital files, which described the overall shape and size of formwork required as well as the geometry of the details needed to join together pieces of foam cut from standard sheets to make larger forms. Gaps between these pieces were filled in with hand-applied foam, and ties and spacers added as needed to stabilise the forms. The concrete was cast with the forms laid flat on the ground slab, then left to cure before the resulting beams were tilted up into place.

The forms' impressions on the concrete surface were in this case left exposed, where they create an interesting motif. Other details of the project produced with the assistance of digital techniques include the milled, transparent urethane gaskets into which the window glazing is set, and the kitchen sink cast in cement using a mould milled from urethane.

Clockwise, from top
Evans House, Enis, Montana, 2002
Digital model; Interior view of wall with sheathing; Plywood flooring joints; Stages in
the installation of the foundations with sheet-metal template; Digital model of exterior
wall construction; Interior view of wall substructure; Exterior view of wall substructure.

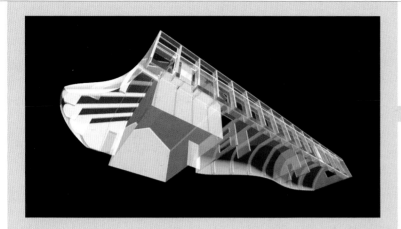

Evans House, Enis, Montana, 2002

For another project, the Evans House, the puzzle-piecing technique used previously for splicing formwork was instead applied to joining sheets of plywood flooring. Other innovative elements of the project included the creation of a full-scale template for the walls' framing, and the construction of an undulating wall with a substructure of PVC tubes threaded through CNC-cut steel ribs.

This wall-construction concept was tested to an extent with digital modelling, and developed to the level of detail required for fabrication of the ribs, but the nondevelopable surface representing the cladding in the model was realised with OSB (oriented strand board) cut into narrow strips, permitting the requisite degree of warping to fit the surface.

A further innovative feature was the use of a template aimed at improving the speed and accuracy of laying out and anchoring the external walls. This template was made by CNC-cutting of sheet steel that included tabs and holes for the attachment of wood framing. Other, more localised templates were used for locating plumbing and electrical fittings embedded in the heated, concrete ground slab. The lessons from trying these techniques were consolidated for use on subsequent projects.

Clockwise, from below (pink border)
Owens House, Broadwater County, Montana, 2002
Exterior view; Digital model of foundation template; Digital model of interior; Stages in the
construction of foundations and reinforced, integrally insulated masonry bearing walls.

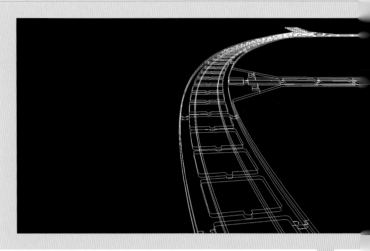

Owens House, Broadwater County, Montana, 2002
The Owens House, for example, had its foundations
built with the assistance of a CNC-cut plywood template
that not only delineated the inner and outer edges of
the exterior masonry walls, but also positioned the
vertical reinforcement bars for the walls and fastened
the edges of the plastic sheets used for forming the
concrete footings (in lieu of traditional carpentry
formwork). Again, gains were realised in the speed and
accuracy of setting these elements, as compared with
a conventional process of surveying and measurement
to establish locations and relationships. In addition,
this approach reportedly allowed the house's siting to
be fine tuned by having the entire template lifted and
shifted to align with a distant mountain-top, the building's
longitudinal axis and the resulting views from inside.

Detailed digital modelling of the project's exterior
and interior, including visible and concealed elements,
allowed the designers to study various functional and
aesthetic relationships. The expertise gained in such
modelling would be applied on other projects as well,
extending to many of the buildings' technical systems
in an effort to gain ever-increasing mastery of
coordination and logistical issues.

An early example of this was in the detailed 3-D
digital models prepared to describe the basement
foundation work on another small house, where it
became apparent, however, that the contractor was
unable (or unwilling) to interrogate the model for
dimensional information as intended, and instead
needed conventional plans and sections printed on
paper in order to work in his accustomed manner.
For one of their current projects, the architects have
modelled volumetrically the components of the
plumbing and electrical distribution systems, both for
design coordination purposes and in order to provide
the digital data used for routing chases directly into
the prefabricated panels of which the walls are built.
Such detailed modelling also permits them to generate
a template for locating interior walls and the fixtures
embedded in the slab – as on earlier projects – but
this time covering the entire footprint of the building.

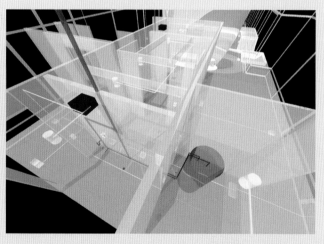

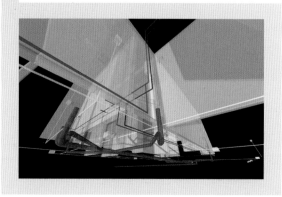

Wooten House, Red Hook, New York, 2004
The architects' exploration of construction systems through digital modelling has also extended to the entire framing of projects such as the Wooten House, which is being built of plywood ribs and sheathing as well as insulated composite panels and some conventional sawn lumber elements. In addition to the design and coordination activities supported by these models, digital fabrication data is once again generated for the plywood and panels. For the more freely sculpted areas of the wall, the architects have again chosen composite panels, but here sliced into curving profiles, turned edgewise and bonded together similarly to the stepped-layered constructions seen in many digital constructions, though in this case with additional machining to remove the steps and smooth the surface. The resulting 'core' is then skinned with bent plywood. Where such large-scale prefabrication is not warranted, and framing (whether CNC-cut or otherwise) is to be assembled on site, the architects have found the digital models to be useful in presenting worm's-eye views readily comprehensible by the carpenters.

The puzzle-piece joining techniques introduced earlier are also undergoing continual development from one project to the next, finding applications in

Wooten House, Red Hook, New York, 2004
Clockwise, from top right
Digital models of framing and sheathing elements for design, coordination and fabrication;
Cutting patterns for structural framing elements.
Cutting patterns for flooring and/or templates.

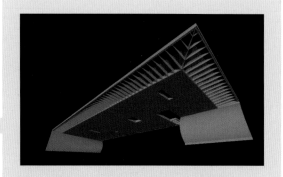

formwork, templating, sheathing, and connections of wood, steel and acrylic elements, whether for wall construction, window framing or furnishings.

Granted, Massie's present facilities – including digital fabrication equipment for model building as well as full-scale construction, all installed in a warehouse large enough to house many of the building elements fabricated by the firm itself – far exceed the extent to which most designers would consider blurring their roles (and commitments) with those of contractors. Yet the firm's degree of interest and engagement in issues of making buildings led to significant results even on the earlier projects when these facilities were not yet under its direct control. Such engagement is certainly within reach for any designer with adequate training, curiosity and initiative. And in any case, it may well be that the role of designer-builder is again in ascendance, at least for projects of a modest scale. Whether builders will increasingly embrace digital techniques so as to take best advantage of the digital data designers can provide remains to be seen. In the interim, digitally produced templates go a long way towards enabling complexity and accuracy for elements that cannot be directly digitally constructed.

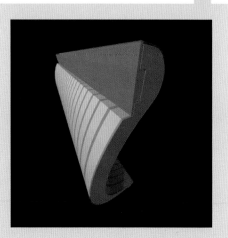

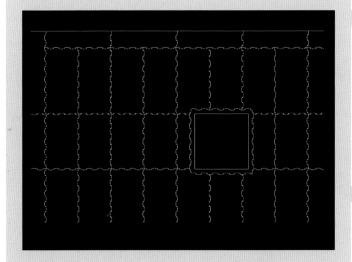

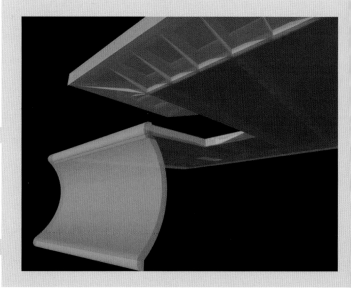

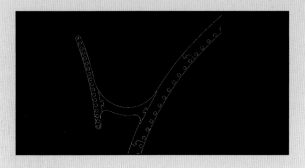

André Chaszar is a contributing editor of *Architectural Design* and a consulting engineer with an independent practice in New York. This article is another in a series of case studies that illustrate the concepts and techniques of CAD/CAM in contemporary architecture, which were first introduced in the initial 'Blurring the Lines' series that appeared in the 2003 volume of *Architectural Design*. These and other texts are collected in a book of the same title to be published by Wiley-Academy in spring 2005.

Below
Villa Monte Rosa, Hong Kong, 2002
A proposed permanent metal frame will give workers both a ladder to reach apartments to install air conditioners and a small platform to stand on while working. A pulley will bring external air conditioners to the apartments. They are then placed within the frame and covered by a system of louvres, which extends the length of the frame. The frame eliminates the need for temporary scaffolding, which is less safe, time-consuming to install and dismantle, and damages the building facade.

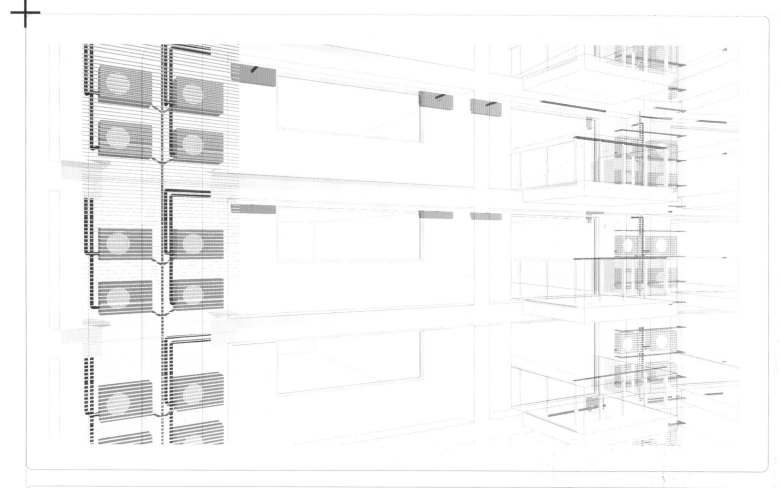

Denise Ho

Architects

Amid the chaotic frenzy of Hong Kong emerges an architectural voice of calm. **Karen A Franck** encounters the work of Denise Ho, an architect who distinguishes herself through her quest for harmony and her careful consideration of her clients' needs.

Hong Kong. The city is not only dense with people but also with sensation. Everywhere there is so much to see, smell, hear and taste. Often, if there is a visual order, which might offer a framework to organise this density of experience, it is not easily apparent. Instead, there is an exuberance of colour, shape and pattern, each item insisting on its own importance, ignoring its neighbours. Neon signs of all shapes in deep jewel-like colours make a dense canopy over a street. Intricate networks of air-conditioning units and snake-like pipes hang off buildings, creating a precarious, chaotic lace of metal. Immensely tall residential towers painted pink, red, orange, pale blue and green forest the hillsides. In the centre, each new corporate tower attempts to imprint its own, ever-taller identity on the skyline.

To this city, calling out for attention at every turn, architect Denise Ho seeks to bring a bit of calm and visual quiet. In sharp contrast to the shrill 'me too, me too' stance of corporate architecture and lavish interiors, she seeks understatement, not only a thoughtful connection to context but an enhancement of it. 'We believe that architecture should bring harmony. In a contextual environment, the design of a piece of architecture is important to its users as much as to the users of the city.' Some of Denise's favourite words are simple, neat, tidy, gentle and subtle; and these adjectives do indeed describe her work. However, her favourite words of all are 'analysis' and 'process', which are just as accurate.

Where some architects, possibly too many, would make a quick assessment of the situation for relatively small-scale projects and immediately propose a design, Ho asks the client (and herself) the first of many questions, uncovering layer upon layer of both problems and potential. What the client may never describe, or even notice, she discovers through keen observation of daily life and routines. What a client may immediately give as a preference becomes the basis for more questions and the material for more insights.

In presenting a client with options along the way, while also explaining what her analysis indicates is the best option, Ho

uncovers yet more information, always making her reasoning fully transparent and always listening carefully to the client's questions and responses. 'Because we always work in a process, we will always work with the client and we are always understanding more and more and more, and coming to the solution together.' In the end, however, she makes only one proposal, clearly generated from analysis and discussion as well as from her own sensibilities and insights: 'I do not think it is fair to ask them to choose. It's like saying: "You choose it. I don't care." And I think we ought to take up certain risks ourselves.'

Observing Daily Life, Creating a Gentle Order

Villa Monte Rosa is a luxury condominium complex of six 20-storey apartment buildings, arranged in a circle, amid mature trees high on a hillside in the Peak district of Hong Kong. Embarking on its renovation, Ho eschewed the immediate paint job (of a bright colour) and mere improvements in appearance: 'Doing a renovation is not about putting on a coat. It's not about going to a party: "What do you fancy tonight?" It's about understanding the problem and the building. There is a lot of character to the building. It has a style and you respect that, and whatever you put on top should improve it.'

Working closely with a devoted committee of residents, the architect gave detailed consideration to the circular garden, above a podium car park, and to the building's facade. At present, in traditional Hong Kong fashion, all households install their own air-conditioning systems in whatever location they choose and with whatever pipes on the exterior are required for that location. The installation and repair of such systems requires temporary scaffolding, which is dangerous and over time destroys the building facade. After input from residents and interviews with

Below
Kiosk and viewing platform, Tsing Ma Bridge, Hong Kong, 1999
A viewing platform with two kiosks, one for refreshments and one for souvenirs, gives visitors a view of the Tsing Ma Bridge through transparent walls and from the surrounding timber deck. Part of one kiosk and the platform, supported by a radiating system of V-shaped steel supports, project out of the hillside, as if floating on the landscape. All services, including air-conditioning units and water tanks, are hidden beneath the platform. Glass walls are flush with the floor, and pebbles keep people away from the glass.

installers, a metal frame was designed for standardising the placement of air-conditioning systems, for making their installation simpler and safer without damage to the building, and for concealing them. The result is a practical solution that eases the lives of residents and installers, an improvement in appearance that reduces the perceived scale of the buildings, and a lesson for the city. Ho comments: 'I think it is improving the city's life. It's an improvement that may not be inside the home, but in the whole society. You begin to see a neater building here, a neater building there.'

The city, particularly the surrounding environment, was again Ho's silent client in her choice of colours for the facade. In order to emphasise the garden and the surrounding greenery, to play down the mass of the building and to avoid clashing with nearby buildings clad in blue and green, she chose olive green and a light off-white for the new tiles. Very

much aware of the bright colours commonly chosen in Hong Kong, Ho notes: 'Everyone is fighting to be noticed but not caring very much about the context. In many places you end up not looking at nature or the greenery or the people – just the buildings. It is very overwhelming.'

Looking Behind the Tender, Finding the Children
Bright colours and lush materials and ornament are common to Hong Kong residential interiors, so much so that visitors to Julien and Pamela Grudzien's newly designed 45th-floor apartment in Kowloon are surprised by the serene whiteness, simple finishes and the feeling of spaciousness in just 2,000 square feet of space. Without knowing why, they may sense the inherent ordering of the space, achieved by an invisible line running the length of the apartment, following the

circulation path. 'That one line defines the curved ceiling, the fittings and how everything in the space is organised. That line organises the air conditioning, the services, the lighting, everything.'

Her attention to the details of daily life and the specific needs of the members of this family is what led the clients to choose Ho for the job. According to Julien Grudzien: 'Of the architects who responded to the tender, Denise was the only one who looked behind it. She was the only one who rang me and asked for a meeting to sit down and elaborate on what I wanted. We spent a couple of hours and then she wanted to come to see where we lived. Later, rather than come round and present, she wanted me to come to the studio to see the lighting – the model – and to test the ceiling. The others – I could tell they were taking out boilerplate ideas. Most of their designs were geared to putting a lot of things in, a lot of build-up, like a grandiose headboard. Not one of them mentioned the children.'

While visiting the family in their former apartment, Ho and her graduate architecture trainee Alice Tsoi Man Ling noticed how much the Grudzien children (one and a half and three years old) ran around, and how much their parents held them. The architects' great empathy with the children then guided several design choices, including the placement of the workspace adjacent to the living space, and not in the master bedroom as Julien had initially requested. Ho explained to Julien: 'We think the children love to come to bed with mom. They love to run around while you are in bed. If you are working there, you are going to lock your kids out? And if the desk is occupying so much space, your kids cannot run around any more.'

There is a space under the stairs where children can hide, a place on the stairs where they can sit and watch the adults below. The bottom shelf of the CD rack and the shoe shelf are low enough for them to reach. Ho emphasises: 'They are always participating.' And at the same time, 'You can't see that the house is designed for children. You don't see big cartoon characters. Instead they can create from their imagination.' Each of the children's bedrooms has a 'grafitti wall' for them to paint on.

The partition wall between the two rooms was removed to make a walk-through closet, forming a private children's realm and another running circuit for them.

Respite from the City
Chick's Chinese Clinic enfolds one in soft light and smooth, nearly seamless surfaces. Upon escaping the visual tumult of the Tin Hua neighbourhood, visitors can enjoy this soothing respite even without an appointment for an acupuncture treatment or a

Diana Wong Art Studio/Residence, Santa Monica, California, US, 2003
Separate living quarters for the artist and her daughter are connected by an internal bridge overlooking the studio, which, like a traditional Chinese courtyard, is a void within the composition. Designed to facilitate the artist's method of working, the studio provides for painting on the floor with large amounts of water that drain off under the floor. The studio opens onto a deck, where painting can also take place.

Chick's Chinese Clinic, Tin Hau, Hong Kong, 2003
To create an open space for yoga or meditation, two acupuncture treatment cubicles have been wheeled back to the outside wall, on the left, and a doctor's work station has been wheeled into the herbal workshop, on the right. A desk provides an outdoor space for patients to enjoy.

Opposite, top right
Chick's Chinese Clinic, Tin Hau, Hong Kong, 2003
View through the acupuncture treatment areas showing the sand-blasted glass doors that doctor pass through to get from one cubicle to the next. Shelving and desk space for the doctor is built into the wall of each cubicle. Swinging doors (on the right) for patients to use are mounted on poles, eliminating the need for door frames, and do not reach the ceiling, increasing the sense of spaciousness.

Below left
Three houses for the Ho family, Ho Sai village, San Shui, 2004
The courtyard, formed by the three buildings, opens to a view of one of the village's fish ponds in the west, also allowing a view of the sunset. Full-height windows/doors on the facades open to the south to catch the summer breeze. The projecting canopy and the vertical brick fins protect against summer heat from the west. The fins also allow the two sets of doors, metal and wood to fold against them when the doors are fully open. Spatially they define pockets of seating areas on the sides of the courtyard +

place of surprising serenity, capturing what Ho calls 'the abstract side of Asian traditions'.

Going Home, Learning from the Local

Ho's father was born and raised in the fishing and farming village of Ho Sai, in San Shui, China, which he left in 1910, eventually settling in Hong Kong. According to village tradition, the family can build a house there for each of the three sons. Ho's mother is eager to do so; without their own houses, she fears the third generation will never return to Ho Sai. Ho never had the opportunity to visit the village with her father, going there for the first time in 1993 after she had attended English boarding schools, completed her Bachelor of Architecture degree at Manchester University, and practised architecture in London. She says now: 'I often wonder what it might have been like when he played his *ye wo* [a vertical musical instrument resembling a violin] in the village forecourt on a moonlit night.' This space, in front of the ancestral hall, is

massage, a herbal remedy or to attend a yoga class. All this is possible in this narrow 1,000-square-foot space on the second floor of an old commercial building. Clients can simply drop by, make themselves a cup of tea, and either read in the small library or sit on the terrace, the partial roof of which creates an intimate outdoor space, shielded from view.

For those receiving an acupuncture treatment, an even more harmonious space is offered in one of three very private 2 x 2 metre cubicles. To enter a cubicle, the patient passes through a remarkable floor-to-ceiling door, hinged top and bottom to a metal pole so that no obtrusive door frame is necessary. The door floats between floor and ceiling, soundlessly swinging open and closed. Between the cubicles, almost invisible doors allow the acupuncturist to pass easily from one cubicle to another. Formed by light maple panels, which also ingeniously incorporate storage space for pillows, blankets and personal belongings as well as a desk, the three cubicles and the treatment beds they house can be wheeled back against the outside wall and their hinged doors folded inwards to hide them. Thus an open space is created for yoga classes, meditation sessions or meetings. The doctor's workstation can also be wheeled into the herbal workshop to create additional floor space.

That the doors and the cubicles are 1.9 metres high and do not reach the ceiling reduces their scale. The continuous surface of the swinging doors and the lack of door frames also increase the sense of spaciousness. A ceiling-mounted light box, running the length of the space, provides diffuse electric light (but hides the fixtures), while floor-to-ceiling window shades bring in diffuse daylight and a shadowy image of the now distant city. The lighting, along with the choice and fashioning of materials – hardly noticeable elements of pale green metal, bamboo floors, maple partitions and doors, and sandblasted glass door panels – creates a

Ho's father was born and raised in the fishing and farming village of Ho Sai, in San Shui, China, which he left in 1910, eventually settling in Hong Kong. According to village tradition, the family can build a house for each of the three sons. Ho's mother is eager to do so; without their own houses, she fears the third generation will never return to Ho Sai.

Top
Three houses for the Ho family, Ho Sai village, San Shui, 2004
The scaffolding, working platform and supports for the concrete formwork for the stair and the floor slab are all based on the same system. The brick wall, under construction here, is used to support the timber studs of a platform that provides a place for workers to stand on while building the upper part of the same wall, and also serves as support for the concrete stair formwork.

Bottom
The main room opens to the courtyard to gain light and view. The room is defined at the back by a brick-finished wall that supports the mezzanine above. The tiny openings at the top of the brick wall, used during construction to support the timber studs and the formwork for the upper floor slab, now become a source of light to the wall behind. An entry opening, at each end of the wall, leads to the back, where the bathroom, kitchen and stair to the mezzanine are located.

At first Ho was eager to build one house with a modern form. But after visiting the village several times and working with the local builders, she 'realised that we cannot dream of using technologies they don't understand'. She also reasoned it would be too expensive and would 'destroy the village'.

where villagers sit around the banyan tree to discuss village matters or tell folk tales.

It was the idea of the village forecourt and outdoor gathering of people in Ho Sai that inspired, in part, Ho's design for the three family houses. Arranged in an L-formation, they define their own forecourt, on the edge of a hill above the village, facing south, as do all of the houses in the village, in order to capture the summer breezes and winter sun. However, unlike traditional houses, the facades facing the forecourt are completely glazed, allowing views of the landscape, with doors that open generously to the forecourt. Tables can be moved into this paved open space, which then becomes an extension of the homes, ideal for large family gatherings. Since it is unlikely that Ho's family in Hong Kong will ever return to live permanently in the houses, they can be small (two are 8 x 8 metres, the other 12 x 8 metres), but at the same time provide space for cousins still residing in the village to use as a library, study space or workshop.

At first Ho was tempted to build one house with a modern form. But after visiting the village several times and working with the local builders, she 'realised that we cannot dream of using technologies they don't understand'. She also reasoned it would be too expensive and would 'destroy the village'. Each of the U-shaped buildings, with its glass wall facing the forecourt, is made of brick, with a pitched roof rising above a single open space and a sleeping loft that shelters a small bathroom and kitchen on the ground floor.

Ho worked closely with the builders, enjoying construction as much as they did, learning from their methods as they learned from her design. In the summer of 2004, she wrote to me: 'The joy of the building process is to see the joy of the workers who learn with us as the building construction goes along. Primitive it seems, but it is highly intelligent in that no unnecessary materials are used. The brick wall being built is also the scaffolding to build the wall above it or to support the formwork for the concrete staircase and the slab above. The thoughts, the planning and care put into building the houses touch me. This is the joy of an architect – working with the people who turn our dream into reality.' And later: 'Light on the textured wall enhances the small space in this very simple house. How often does an architect in a city think of light as a source of inspiration when the maximum GFA [gross floor area] becomes the goal of design?'

And we might ask, expectantly: What will Ho be able to bring from her experience in Ho Sai to the many new projects she and her growing staff are now undertaking (including a centre for the organisation Against Child Abuse in Macau, eight new houses in Shatin and a new private house in Sai Kung)?

Karen Franck is an environmental psychologist who teaches architecture and social science courses at the New Jersey Institute of Technology in Newark, US. She is a frequent contributor to *Architectural Design*, and is the guest-editor of two issues on architecture and the culture of food: *Food and Architecture* (Nov/Dec 2002) and *Food + the City* (to be published in May 2005).

Left, top and bottom
Village Houses, Shatin, Hong Kong, 2005
Eight buildings will be constructed in pairs of two, allowing six flats to share
each external stair. While the four stair systems are the same, differences
in colour, window placement, or the addition of a small balcony individualise
the pairs, giving residents a sense of the personality of their homes.

Right
Alice Tsoi Man Ling (left) and Denise Ho (right).

Denise Ho

Architects

Resumé

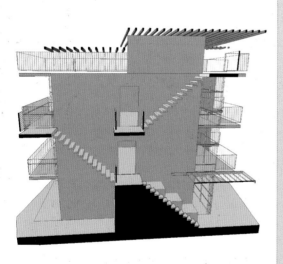

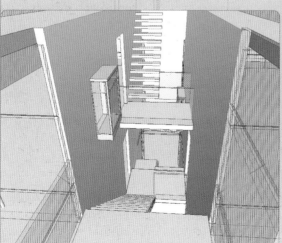

1996	Established Denise Ho Architects, Hong Kong
1997	Chan Residence renovation, Bonham Road, Hong Kong Tong Residence, Avenida Da Republica, Macau
1998	Ho Residence, Caine Road, Hong Kong
1999	Kiosks and Viewing Platform, Tsing Ma Bridge, Hong Kong
2002	Proposal for Villa Monte Rosa renovation, Stubbs Road, Hong Kong Trellises along waterfront near Provident Center, Hong Kong
2003	Chick's Chinese Clinic, Tin Hau, Hong Kong Grudzien Apartment, Kowloon, Hong Kong Diana Wong Art Studio/Residence, Santa Monica, California, US
2004	Three houses for the Ho family, Ho Sai village, San Shui, China
Ongoing	Against Child Abuse centre, Macau Grand Garden renovation, South Bay, Hong Kong Garden Terrace renovation, Old Peak Road, Hong Kong Prototype design for minibus stand, central Hong Kong Village houses, Shatin, Hong Kong Residential redevelopment, Kowloon City, Hong Kong Holden Residence renovation, Hong Lok Yuen, Hong Kong

www.denisehoarchitects.com

Below
Il Sottomarine – the Submarine House – or the Villa Taddei, San Domenico al
Fiesole, Italy. Designed by Leonardo Savioli and Domenico Santi.

The Submarine on the Hill

Our intrepid autotravellers, David Heathcote and Sue Barr, continue their quest across Europe in search of that illusive holy grail – the 1970s house. They remain undeterred, or almost, by the number that are hidden and shuttered, with absentee owners.

There is a joke about asking directions; the punchline is: 'I wouldn't start from here.' One of the worst ways to write any book is to propose new photography, especially if you're the authors. Doh!

Long ago we accepted we weren't the sharpest tools in the box. So perhaps we can be forgiven for thinking new images are better than recycling archive footage, especially in the case of modern architecture where buildings are shot at the moment of birth surrounded by nothing but sheets of earth and umbilical roads. What we wanted was maturity, context, patina, architecture vérité, *Domus* Dogma etc, etc. Another mistake was an interest in buildings of the 1970s or, more specifically, houses, single houses, villas, examples of pure aesthetics constricted by an archetype – big sculptures even.

We had to decide where to look first and, by fortune or subliminal choice, we found a nexus of '70s-ness between Ticino and Tuscany, which sounded nice. We knew it was a

good idea because of the general disdain at our dilettante pursuit of meretricious trendiness – nothing is more reassuring than the judgement of academics.

With a handful of photocopies from 1970s archi-mags, we set off for the Continent. Despite the large number of 1970s houses that lurk unnoticed in Britain we felt this was too insular, too Little England. The reason for our national parochialism – an inability to imagine that there is any other language – was no less true of us; we faced our research with little information and little ability to gain more. We had pictures of 1970s houses and we were going to find them. Besides, we were bored.

I will skip the journey except to mention our escape from a vertiginous and snowy death in the Alps, and a shunt, a real hairdresser's accident, travelling south on the A1 (Italy) – but these are details.

Left
Angelo Andina house, Losone, Ticino, Switzerland, 1967.

Right
Casa Bianchi, Riva san Vitale, Ticino, Switzerland. Designed by Mario Botta, 1971–3.

Left
Angelo Andina house, Losone, Ticino, Switzerland, 1967.

Right
Casa Bianchi, Riva san Vitale, Ticino, Switzerland. Designed by Mario Botta, 1971–3.

The architectural press generally is a bit vague on details about locations of private houses, usually resorting to rather gnomic descriptions like, 'summer house on Lake Como', but we felt that the buildings we chose were so distinctive you couldn't miss them. Well, we didn't know how big Lake Como is, or that what looks like a littoral road on a map disguises a massive hinterland of strand, or that in many cases you can't really see what's on the other bank because, in our mind's eye, we thought 'lakes? Ullswater'. Heading for Switzerland, Ticino to be more exact, we were in for another shock. In the UK Modern houses stand out because they are rare; in Ticino, as everyone else knows, the ground is stiff with every variety of Modernity, Postmodernity and general contemporaneity. This pulled us up a bit, but didn't daunt us, as our houses were very distinctive. The first was a glass box by the Maggia River, the second a tower on a sloping site by a smallish lake with a metal bridge leading to it surrounded by nothing, and the third we knew was in the village of Torricella.

We tried the Valle Maggia and found nothing corresponding to our picture all the way up to the village of Maggia, even though we were now used to sifting through thousands of fantastic houses that were all neighbours. The road in fact seemed to make it impossible to fit a house between it and the river, and a railway ran on the other side of the road – we thought about going home. We sulkily photographed a nice house in Maggia, which later surprised us by being a very early Botta (we had a bit of a downer on Botta – too 1980s) and went to the tourist information office where the very attractive lady on the counter knew exactly where our house was as she walked her dog on the opposite bank.

The opposite bank, which was pretty downmarket for Ticino, turned out to be an archifeast in itself, full of the architectural equivalents of R.V.s (like in the 1970s TV show *The Rockford Files*).

Everywhere was Le Corb Lite, with Ronchampesque double garages next to Frank Lloyd Wright bungalows. But one building really stood out: a brown villa with circular picture windows covered by orange shutters. We had died and gone to '70s heaven: Huggy Bear's Swiss retreat! After a bit of research it turned out that this is a house by Angelo Andina, and isn't 1970s at all, dating from 1967 – damn!

Like a couple of twitchers after eating a Twix, we returned to our task almost opposite, on the other bank of our house. The original picture didn't do it justice, and this is always the case with archive photography, usually because it is only concerned with the building and form, and not its context and, of course, lens distortion. Though the original image was good in black and white, the

building was gloriously pink – like a gay fragment of the Centre Pompidou, it stood out from the acres of tasteful form. In fact, it is the only pink thing in Switzerland. Funnily, once you've found your house, the best way to find out who owns it is not to consult any guide except the *Swiss White Pages,* where the owner's phone number will be for certain, along with their profession. Guides are chiefly concerned with the architects – who are also in the phone book! – and they are hard to get to and can't always get you in. This took us some months to figure out.

When we finally visited the house, which was, unusually, lived in by the architect, we found out why it was invisible from the road – the roof was his lay-by parking place and just looked like a part of the road with a car on it. The house itself was essentially a glass cube with total internal flexibility. The architect had, using basic building-yard stuff, created movable floors, stairs, walls, and wide sliding doors as well as much of the furniture. He showed us a picture of the original mauve-hued abstract floor painting, and how he had made a hot tub with a view of the river from a section of massive concrete conduit. Out back was a sculpture studio and an insulated glazed soundbox for his son's drums, and a ceramic studio for his wife. It was fantastic – the whole structure was well crafted, economical, built by local workmen out of basic materials and, yet, much more, it was warm, light, spacious, comfortable, livable, personal, adaptable and felt like the locus of constant creativity – we liked it. It had the individualism and optimism we were looking for, combining old-fashioned Modernist concerns with craft and detail with a very unmodern desire for classical height and geometry (as opposed to horizontality) and a very unarchitectural regard for cheap ecology, change, adaptability, and a sort of fuzzy *Big Lebowski* laid-back generosity.

After this we were dreading the power-dressed Botta villa near Lugano, which is very chic in places. But we were wrong about Botta – his villa had all the same optimism, comfort and approachable style as the Valle Maggia house. What in all the archive images appeared to be a research centre for Nazi dentists, or a gangster refuge, was, 30 years on, as mellow and elegant as a temple at Stourhead. As a house it was very ordinary, a real home, and not overly stylish, as many now fall prey to, yet at the same time a strong architectural statement. It has, for instance, a big wood-fire set in a surround of ochre-toned polished plaster that you can sit right next to, low down, by a glass door that opens onto the surrounding garden – on one of the upper verandas, which is room sized, you can look out over the lake to an ancient church in any weather, out of the wind. Nice.

Full of optimism we headed for Tuscany because at Fiesole was a fantastic house, the Villa Taddei, which is both sculpture and house, a clockwork orange. Following our established method, we drove to Fiesole and went to the tourist information office. Unfortunately, in Italy, these places are work-placement opportunities for attractive but sulky girls where they learn to be uninformative in the same way that Alitalia stewards are trained as partnerships in the dumb and dumber method. Bitter?

We did find out, by buying a map, that San Domenico al Fiesole is a different place from Fiesole, and down the hill. San Domenico al Fiesole was so small we drove through it twice and found it only by asking where it was at a bar. We were in it. Did they know the Villa Taddei (they spoke English, too)? No. But when we showed them the picture they did know. The house was 100 metres along the road that ran past the side of the bar. We had seen it but we weren't looking, if you know what I mean.

Unlike Switzerland, Italy is superficially social, but this ends at the beginning of wealthy residential streets. We could see the house and it was all we had hoped, like a shuttered concrete model of a human heart – very Archigram – but it lay behind high walls and blank gates. We tried a paparazzi shot standing on a near wall topped by a huge chain-link fence – well, one of us did, and not the writer. The light was falling, the camera was a standard lens, the building far off as a pack of Dobermans attacked through the fence and the security lights came on. All I had time to do was take a look at the nameplate on the Villa Taddei. It said 'Il Sottomarine'.

Back in England we tried the phone book. There were three Taddeis in San Domenico al Fiesole, but none lived in or even knew the Villa Taddei. And there were no Sottomarines listed. However, the son of one of the architects, who had both died, was also an architect and told us the house was for sale and that he would arrange a visit for us. When we got there it was apparently 'impossible' after all. We went to look at the villa again; just out of reach. Looking at the nameplate I saw that there were two handwritten names by two bells. Then the penny dropped. Sottomarine wasn't the owner of the Villa Taddei. It had been renamed Il Sottomarine because it looked a bit like the Yellow Submarine. Doh! Still, we know who lives there now. ⚿

David Heathcote and Sue Barr are currently working on *The 70s House* for Wiley-Academy's 'Interior Angles' series, scheduled for publication in early 2005. Heathcote's book *Barbican: Penthouse Over the City*, with photography by Sue Barr, was published by Wiley-Academy in June 2004. David Heathcote is a design writer and historian. Sue Barr is a photographer and tutor at the Architectural Association in London. Widely published in the international architectural press, Barr has also extensively photographed authentic London café culture for *London Caffs* (author Edwin Heathcote), published by Wiley-Academy in September 2004.

Book Review

New London Interiors
by Kieran Long

ISBN 1858942373 £29.95
Hardback 240 pages
300 colour illustrations
Merrell, 2004

Design City: Tokyo
by Masaaki Takahashi

ISBN 470093641 £34.99
Hardback 216 pages
300 colour illustrations
Wiley-Academy, 2004

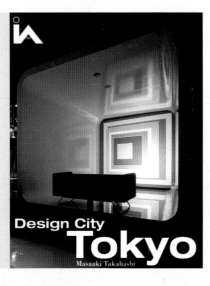

London has not always been at the forefront of interior design. Even in the 1960s, when it was one of the style capitals of the world, the innovations in interiors were limited compared to those in fashion and art, and for the following two decades its design scene went into decline. But in March 1997, Vanity Fair announced that London was 'swinging again' – and this time, interior design had caught up. From the 'London minimalism' of the early 1990s to the more outrageous confections of the last few years, London style has quickly diversified, and inventive interiors are no longer limited to exclusive settings. Over the same period, Tokyo has undergone a more steady transformation into the iconic style city that it is today. After spending some years looking to the West, Japanese designers came to recognise the value of their home-grown culture for inspiration, giving them a cross-cultural freedom which has allowed Tokyo to become a city unlike any other. Today, here as in London, even office buildings, traditionally the most staid of environments, are branded to the hilt, and retail outlets offer not just a showcase for a product but a complete lifestyle experience.

These two cities, now among the world's most vibrant design hotspots, have inspired two sumptuous new books – *New London Interiors* by Kieran Long (Merrell, £29.95) and *Design City: Tokyo* by Masaaki Takahashi (Wiley-Academy, £34.99). Following their respective introductory chapters setting the scene of design in these cities since the 1960s, the core part of each book comprises selections of the best recent interiors organised according to type, the Tokyo book also extending in some cases to full buildings. Glancing at just one of these sections is enough to give an idea of the extraordinary variety that exists in interior design today, and the spread of the sections themselves – covering bars and restaurants, shops, leisure and fitness facilities, workplaces and homes, among others – demonstrates how style has pervaded all aspects of life. Internationally famous names are featured alongside fresh new talent and more local practices, and no-holds-barred extravagances alongside more frugal creations that are no less inventive.

Both writers are passionate about their home cities, which they clearly know inside out. Their descriptions concisely set the projects in context and, beyond that, reveal a personal familiarity which makes them all the more engaging, evoking atmosphere so that even the remote reader can have a sense of the real experience of these interior environments. The quality of the photography in both books is consistently high. Whilst the London projects are limited to two pages each, those in the Tokyo book extend to up to eight pages, so that Long's book gives a more wide-ranging snapshot whilst Takahashi's delves deeper.

The Tokyo book has a number of welcome additional features which will be especially useful to those who want to see the projects for themselves. Dates and locations are clearly picked out, and a listing provides addresses and contact information for all projects that are accessible to the public. A further section giving an overview of the history and design characteristics of each of the districts of Tokyo is an added bonus to anyone planning to visit. Introductions to each themed section add an extra level of information, and the well-considered captions are also helpful, both in enhancing the reader's understanding of the spaces and in making it possible to dip into the book more easily. It may be the lack of captioning in the London book that has allowed some photographs of Future Systems' Selfridges interiors to appear masquerading as their Oxford Street New Look, but this slip-up should not deter the potential buyer as the overall quality of the content and presentation is high. ⧋+

Abigail Grater